Scary Gross & Weird STORIES

from the BIBLE

Bloody Tent Pegs, Disembodied Fingers, and Suicidal Pigs...

D1591686

the Truths Buried in the Bizarre

13 BIBLE LESSONS FOR TEENAGERS

Loveland, Colorado
www.group.com

Group resources actually work!

This Group resource helps you focus on **"The 1 Thing®"**— a life-changing relationship with Jesus Christ. "The 1 Thing" incorporates our **R.E.A.L.** approach to ministry. It reinforces a growing friendship with Jesus, encourages long-term learning, and results in life transformation, because it's:

Relational
Learner-to-learner interaction enhances learning and builds Christian friendships.

Experiential
What learners experience through discussion and action sticks with them up to 9 times longer than what they simply hear or read.

Applicable
The aim of Christian education is to equip learners to be both hearers and doers of God's Word.

Learner-based
Learners understand and retain more when the learning process takes into consideration how they learn best.

Group

Scary, Gross & Weird Stories from the Bible

Copyright © 2008 Group Publishing, Inc.

Visit our Web site: **www.group.com**

Credits

Contributing Authors: Joy-Elizabeth Lawrence, Jim Miller, Siv Ricketts, Summer Salomonsen, and Christina Schofield
Editor: Kate Holburn
Senior Developer: Roxanne Wieman
Project Manager: Scott M. Kinner
Chief Creative Officer: Joani Schultz
Copy Editor: Michael Van Schooneveld
Art Director: Jeff Storm
Interior Designer/Print Production Artist: Jay Smith-Juicebox Designs
Cover Art Director: Jeff Storm
Cover Designer: Jeff Storm
Production Manager: Peggy Naylor

Library of Congress Cataloging-in-Publication Data

Scary, gross & weird : bloody tent pegs, disembodied fingers, and suicidal pigs ... the truths buried in the bizarre : 13 Bible lessons for teenagers. -- 1st American pbk. ed.
    p. cm.
  ISBN 978-0-7644-3698-7 (pbk. : alk. paper) 1. Church work with teenagers. 2. Bible stories. 3. Christian teenagers--Religious life. I. Group Publishing. II. Title: Scary, gross, and weird.
  BV4447.S24 2008
  220.071'2--dc22
                              2007038353

ISBN 978-0-7644-3698-7
10 9 8 7 6 5 4 3 2 1   17 16 15 14 13 12 11 10 09 08

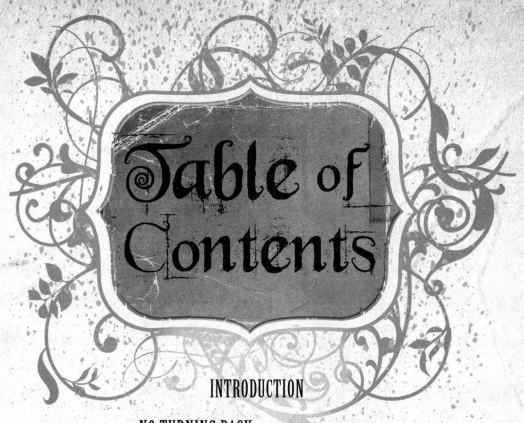

Table of Contents

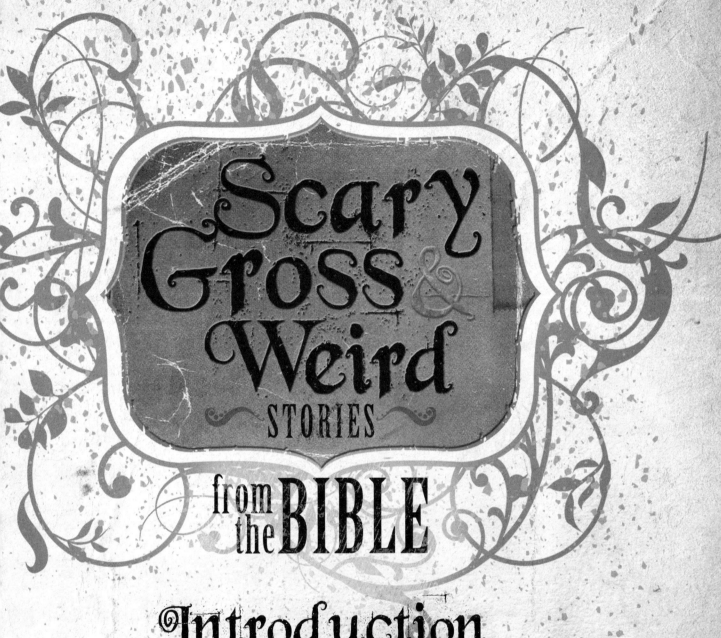

Scary Gross & Weird STORIES from the BIBLE

Introduction

Most of the youth in your ministry undoubtedly know the familiar, likely Bible accounts. They've read them dozens of times. Adam and Eve in Eden, God calling Samuel, Esther's courage, Saul's transformation into Paul. Of course, these are amazing highlights from the story of God's loving relationship with his people. But what about the unfamiliar characters? The unlikely accounts? Do your students know just how offbeat and uncomfortable some parts of the Bible can be? How terrifying? How…dare we say it…**weird?**

Scary, Gross, & Weird Stories from the Bible explores 13 bizarre true stories with a can't-look-away approach. Now, we understand very well that your teenagers probably won't be shocked by what they find in these passages; they've become immune to drama and gore and the grotesque like no generation before. However, they may have never before associated any of that with God's Word. In fact, their view of the Bible might run more along these lines: sterilized, predictable, safe, dull. So here's your opportunity to surprise them, shake the faith dialogue up a bit, and guide them through some provocative, life-transforming experiences. Think of these 13 decidedly non-safe stories as the back-alley accounts of the Bible…where God's light often shines the brightest.

Your students will be surprised and intrigued by the strange things (and people) in these passages—but keep in mind that strangeness isn't the focus. We're not helping your students encounter weirdness for weirdness' sake (or grossness for grossness' sake—you get the picture). Instead, the goal of these unique encounters with unexpected, unsettling stories is *solely* to show your teenagers more of who God is. And, well, God is pretty unexpected and unsettling. Not to mention utterly creative. So creative, in fact, that he included a lot of head-scratching, cringe-inducing, and downright disturbing stories in his Word. And each one reveals something about God and what it means to be in an intimate, redeeming relationship with Jesus Christ.

We've designed each of the 13 studies in this resource to achieve that very purpose: to equip your students to *really* dig into fresh, startling Scripture passages…so they'll be astounded by our extraordinary Creator and Savior, and moved to love and serve him with their lives.

To that end, here's a full breakdown of how we've built this resource.

Each fun, practical, and peculiar study centers around one **main theme** that is highlighted through every experience and discussion. This main theme helps teenagers grow spiritually and live in ways that glorify God. A detailed **supply list** and **preparation and setup** guide give you everything you need to get ready. The materials are generally easy-to-find, but consider borrowing from congregation members whatever you don't already have.

✹ **THE GOO…**The study starts with a bang: something both active and interest-capturing to pull teenagers into the study's tone—and introduce the main theme.

✹ **THE GUTS…** Here's the meat of the study: a fascinating, in-depth exploration of the Bible study. The storytelling is dramatic and innovative, emphasizing the scary, gross, or weird aspects of the story (think story time around the campfire). You'll also explore the theme and dig into Scripture for context and other supporting passages.

✹ **THE GRIT…**In this final part of the study, you'll help guide students to a personal connection with the theme. This might involve an on-the-edge challenge, an interactive experience, or a simple contemplative response. Whatever the activity, it will lead naturally to…

✹ **THE GEL…** Where students are given a clear opportunity to make practical commitments for living out what they've discovered. These application steps are relevant, doable, and meaningful.

IN EACH STUDY, YOU'LL ALSO FIND:

🦇 **pit•tip.** Scattered throughout, these tips give you helpful hints and suggestions for specific activities or situations.

🦇 **Cleaning Up.** This is an additional collection of open-ended, thought-provoking questions. Use all or some of them to complement—or even replace—the debriefing questions for each activity. You can guide students through this section all together or form smaller discussion groups for more intimate dialogue.

🦇 One **photocopiable piece.** Your students will interact with this handout in some way during the study, whether as script, guide, map, journal, or list.

🦇 A **creative prayer.** In perhaps the most profound moments of the session, teenagers will connect with God through a unique prayer practice.

🦇 An **interesting quote.** Share this funny, strange, or informative blurb with your students—or just store it away for later.

Media Infusion. Here's a brief optional activity for watching a movie clip, listening to a song, or mining the Internet for a surprising spiritual link. You can fit this serious, offbeat, or poignant idea into the study wherever you'd like an added punch.

Believe It or Not. Check out this real-life gross, weird, or scary story that relates to the Bible story your group is exploring. Share it with your students as a fun bonus before, during, or after the study. Or, better yet, have a volunteer read it aloud.

Mixing It Up. This box highlights two or three other Bible stories that contain a similar "weirdness" or touch on the same theme. You can plan to read these together as a group or suggest that your students explore them on their own.

Bizarre Bonus. Here's a powerful, take-it-to-the-next-level idea for students—either to do outside of the group or together if you have time. This is an over-the-top experience that relates to the Bible story and theme you're exploring. Consider it a cool-but-weird challenge (that should take more time and prep work) to drive the discovery home.

REMEMBER: You know your teenagers best, so please use this resource in ways that fit your group, space, time, and individual needs. The activities, statements, and questions are simply tools to help you facilitate meaningful experiences—so feel free to follow them word-for-word, adapt liberally, or springboard to your own ideas.

While we don't really know (though we eagerly anticipate) what will come from your teenagers' encounters with these stories, this resource does come with a few guarantees. First, it will be relevant for students of various ages, backgrounds, and faith levels. Second, it will work with groups of three, 100, and anywhere in between. Third, it will challenge teenagers to a deeper, more mature relationship with Jesus Christ. These things we promise—the rest is up to you and your students. Our prayer is you'll undergo a weird, wild, and wonderful adventure…

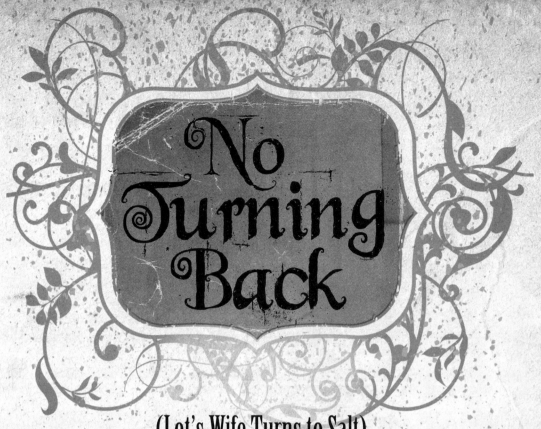

No Turning Back

(Lot's Wife Turns to Salt)

BIBLE STORY: GENESIS 18:16-33

THEME: THE PERFECT CHARACTER OF GOD
Subtopics: Obedience, Justice, Perseverance, Following Through, Family

Students will learn how God did what he said he would do when Lot's wife disobeyed, but also how God rescued Lot and his children. Students will discover that God graciously rescues and justly does what he says he will do. They'll also be challenged to obey God fully, even when they don't understand his plan.

SUPPLIES NEEDED:
- a new toothbrush for everyone
- a can of vegetable shortening
- a foam cup for everyone
- water
- paper towels
- a small prize for everyone (piece of candy, soda, dollar bill, etc.)
- pencils
- Bibles
- 10 pieces of paper
- mirror (the biggest you can find)
- glass cleaner
- (optional) salty snacks
- (optional) computer(s) with an Internet connection

PREPARATION AND SETUP:
- Fill a big bowl with the prizes you've designated. Label it "The Big Bowl of Fabulous Prizes."
- Photocopy a "Mad Lib" handout (p. 8) for every two or three students.

Greet everybody as they arrive. Start with an ultimate challenge.

SAY Anyone who competes in this toothbrushing contest will receive an awesome prize from The Big Bowl of Fabulous Prizes. Everybody participating will load their brushes up with some of this shortening and brush their teeth as long as they can. The person lasting the longest can choose *two* prizes out of the Big Bowl of Fabulous Prizes and will be considered to be *double* fabulous. Let's do it!

Help volunteers load their brushes (or fingers) up with the lardy goop, give the signal to start, and see who can last the longest. Distribute foam cups everyone can spit into when they are done. When it comes time to reward those who participated and proclaim a winner, do something surprising: award the fabulous prizes to those who didn't participate. Cheerfully grant the top prize to the biggest no-funner of the bunch. Give students a moment to protest, and then:

ASK
- How mad are you that I didn't follow through with what I promised?
- Why is it a big deal to be trustworthy?
- What would the world be like without justice?

➡ *At this point, you might want to distribute prizes to everyone before full-on anarchy erupts.*

SAY I can't begin to imagine what it would be like if God didn't do the stuff he said he would do—good stuff and punishment stuff. We couldn't trust anything in the Bible. We'd be left to guess about everything—could we trust him to save us when we die? It's a great thing to see his mercy woven through the pages of the Bible, but it's also pretty comforting to see how he kept his promises time and again, and did what he said he would, even at times when it must have grieved him. Today's story is a good example of both God's mercy and his justice.

pit·tip

Buy cheap toothbrushes in bulk or look for deals in dollar stores. If your group is too large or you just can't swing the expense, have students use the "finger-brushing" method.

BELIEVE IT OR NOT

In Oregon, a seventh grade long-distance runner was chased by a deer who began using him as a human salt lick. Kevin Cox told reporters that the incident was "funny…but a little scary," too.

Bizarre Bonus

Here's a crazy idea to do together after the study.

Load up a table in the room with all kinds of salty junk food. Have everyone partner up. While one person keeps their eyes shut, the other one should chew a mouthful of food, then see if their partner can identify it by looking at the mush in their partner's mouth. Take it a step further with two- or three-food-combo challenges. Use the goofy salt-connection to segue into a discussion about what it means to follow Jesus.

The Guts...

Distribute the photocopies of the "Mad Lib" handout (p. 8). Have everybody form pairs or trios. One person in the group should fill in the mad lib using their partners' suggestions. Then, when all the blanks have been filled, groups can read the goofy story together.

Once everyone has finished, ask the groups to find Genesis 18:16-33. Give them enough time to read the verses among themselves, then prompt them with these questions to talk about in their groups.

ASK · What surprised you most when you read this?

· What did you learn about God's mercy in these verses?

SAY Unfortunately, there weren't even ten good people in the town of Sodom. Instead, God found only Lot and his family. He told them he would lead them out of the city so they wouldn't get barbecued with the others. Let's pick up the story there. Keep reading at Genesis 19:15-29.

➔ *Give students a few minutes to finish reading the Bible story. Then:*

> ### MEDIA INFUSION (optional)
> Search news Web sites, magazines, or newspapers for examples of famous people who faced indictment or were sentenced for breaking the law. Discuss the punishment they received or didn't receive, and talk about whether or not it was fair. (If you need ideas, here are some names your teenagers might be familiar with: Paris Hilton, O.J. Simpson, Martha Stewart, Scooter Libby.)

ASK
- What do you think caused Lot's wife to turn back?
- How would you label her punishment: appropriate, too harsh, just plain weird, or something else? Explain your answer.
- What can you know about God based on this story's ending?

If you don't have access to a big mirror, or if your group is just too big, give each student a piece of aluminum foil they can smear up with Crisco and write on. (Faster clean-up, too.)

Use your can of vegetable shortening from earlier to smear up a large mirror. Spread it evenly until the whole surface is covered. This can be done quickly, right in front of students as you talk.

SAY Mercy is a great thing when we are the ones getting off easy. But something inside us stirs when justice isn't served. It is that quality of justice within God that required a punishment for sin: we all mess up and disobey him—a capital offense punishable by death. The mercy of God came by way of his perfect son, Jesus, who made payment on our behalf by dying a terrible death to save us from hell. If you don't fully understand what Jesus did for you on the cross, please come and talk with me after our study.

SAY I want you guys to think about God's perfect character. Write some qualities that describe him with your finger onto this glass. Let's start by writing two we've talked about today.

➡️ *Use your finger to write "just" and "merciful" into the grease, then give students a chance to crowd around the mirror and write their thoughts in the shortening. Provide paper towels for clean-up.*

Read 1 Corinthians 13:12 aloud:

"Now we see but a poor reflection as in a mirror; then we shall see face to face. Now I know in part; then I shall know fully, even as I am fully known."

SAY It is a challenge to love and serve God when we can't see him, hear him, or touch him. We can only see bits and glimpses of his character in Scripture and in the things around us. God's faithfulness and consistency are crucial to our understanding of who he is. He has to do what he promises, even if it breaks his heart and ours. It is also obvious through Scripture and his plan for saving us that he has tremendous mercy and compassion on us. This verse we read has a neat promise. One day, we are going to see God face to face and know him the way he knows us, through and through.

➡ *(At this point, use the glass cleaner to clean the mirror off, showing a distinction between making out only a fuzzy description of God, to seeing clearly.)*

SAY Until that time, it is important to read his Word and learn what we can about who he is. Just think about these questions silently—you don't need to answer them out loud.

ASK · How does God's character differ from your own?

· In what ways has God been merciful to you?

· How has he proved to you that he means what he says?

· How does this change the way you think, feel, and connect with Jesus?

The Gel...

Offer your teenagers three challenges to help them better know and understand God's character:

· Keep a running list of every example you find in your Bible reading of God's justice and of his mercy.

- Identify one God-like characteristic you will focus on every day of the coming week.
- Spend five minutes before bed just being quiet with God, and see if you learn anything about him during that time.

 Ask students to pray with a partner by simply naming aloud different aspects of God's character and thanking him for who he is. Here are a few to get them started: God is merciful. God is just. God is kind. God is holy. God is good…

After several moments, close your meeting with a prayer.

SAY God, thank you for taking the guesswork out of things. Because you consistently do what you say, we know we can trust your words to be true. That gives us hope because we are counting on your mercy and holding onto your promise of help and salvation. Thanks for being faithful and reliable and, above all, merciful toward us. Amen.

Don't Pee on
My Leg
and Tell Me
It's Raining
—Title of book by Judge
Judy Sheindlin

BEGIN CLEANING UP

CLEANING UP

Here are some additional open-ended, thought-provoking questions. Use all or some of them to complement—or even replace—the debriefing questions for any of the activities in this study. You can guide students through this section all together, or form smaller discussion groups for more intimate dialogue.

- How would you rate today's story on a weirdness scale of 1 to 10?

- Sum today's Bible story up in one sentence.

- How would you define justice?

- How would you define mercy?

- Why is it frustrating when someone doesn't get what they deserve?

- Name a time you were relieved that you didn't get something you deserved.

- How would the world be different if God wasn't merciful?

- How would the world be different if God wasn't just?

- Name one thing you can do, starting today, to be a more merciful person.

- Tell God thanks, in your own words, for his flawless character.

pit·tip

Consider writing the "Cleaning Up" questions onto pieces of paper, one question per page. Beforehand, tape the pages to the wall or onto the table. At this point in the study, distribute pencils and have teenagers walk around to all the different questions and write their answers on the paper.

For huge groups, write the questions onto ten pieces of poster board so there is more room for writing. For really huge groups, make two or three posters for every question so students aren't all bunched up trying to write on the same ten boards.

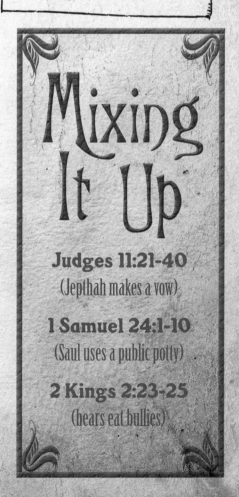

Mixing It Up

Judges 11:21-40
(Jepthah makes a vow)

1 Samuel 24:1-10
(Saul uses a public potty)

2 Kings 2:23-25
(bears eat bullies)

7

The town of Sodom was a [_____], [_____] town. People
                  WORD FOR BAD   WORD FOR **REALLY** BAD

there were [_____]-ing constantly. They ignored God and
              A SIN

broke the most important rule: [_____]. God was fed up.
                       A RULE

Abraham pleaded with God to spare Sodom. If God could find some good guys

there, perhaps he could rain down [_____] instead of fire
                          SOMETHING FLUFFY AND NICE

and brimstone.

    "God, if you find 50, or 40, or 30, or 20, or 10 guys half as good as [_____],
                                                   A NICE PERSON IN YOUR GROUP

would you please not wipe out Sodom with a big fireball?" God agreed. Unfortunately, God

only found one good guy there. Only Lot and his family would be spared.

    They were given special instructions: Pack the [_____] and the
                                           A NECESSITY ITEM

[_____]. Don't forget the [_____
           A BREAKFAST CEREAL

_____].
SOMETHING YOU'D WISH YOU HAD IF YOU WERE ON THE SHOW **LOST**

    They would be led out of their hometown by angels, and then,

"[_____]!" Total destruction! "[_____]!"
  A LOUD SOUND   **AN EXCLAMATION**

    "Whatever you do, don't turn back," Lot's family was sternly warned. But Lot's

wife didn't listen. Did she go back to turn off the [_____]?
                                            AN ELECTRICAL APPLIANCE

Only God knows. The moment she looked back, she was turned to a pile of salt. God keeps

his promises—the ones we want kept, and those we choose to ignore.

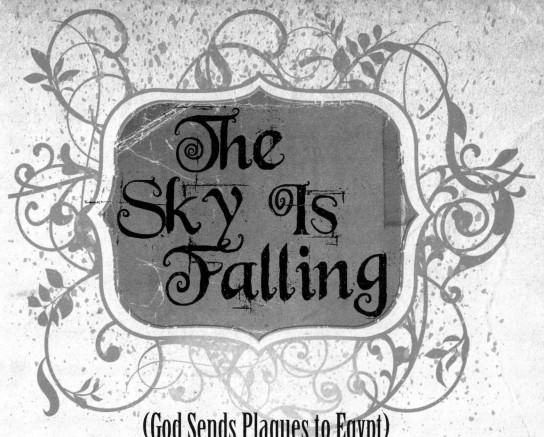

The Sky Is Falling

(God Sends Plagues to Egypt)

BIBLE STORY: EXODUS 7:14–12:30

THEME: ULTIMATE TRUST

Subtopics: Justice, Freedom, God's Sovereignty, God's Children

Students will study the story of the plagues of Egypt and learn that they can trust God even in the midst of huge obstacles.

SUPPLIES NEEDED:
- a fine-tipped marker for each person
- (optional) a live frog in a portable container
- a few handfuls of the kinds of rubber spiders or insects that are available at toy stores, discount stores, party supply stores, and online (such as www.orientaltrading.com)
- sealable bags
- water
- yellow food coloring

- (optional) There may also be a photo on the Web of a plague of locusts flying in front of the pyramids of Giza. Search for "plague of locusts, Giza" and see if you can find it.
- a can of alphabet soup and a can opener for every five students
- a lot of newspaper
- several rolls of paper towels (or a nearby sink)
- (optional) a DVD of the movie *The Prince of Egypt*, DVD player, and TV

(continued on next page)

SUPPLIES NEEDED (*continued*):

- 10 images either in a computer slide presentation or printed out (you can find all of these by typing them into an Internet search engine):
  1. a picture of the Nile river
  2. a picture of a frog (or a lot of frogs)
  3. a picture of a louse (close-up)
  4. a picture of a swarm of flies
  5. a picture of a dead cow (yes, they're online, and no, it doesn't have to be too graphic)
  6. a picture of boiling water (boils, get it?)
  7. a picture of hail
  8. a picture of a swarm of locusts
  9. a picture of dark clouds
  10. a picture of a tombstone

PREPARATION AND SETUP:

- Make a copy of the handout (p. 18) for every student.
- Put several rubber spiders or insects in resealable bags filled with water. For added effect, put yellow food coloring in the water.
- Print out hard copies of the ten images above or make them into a slide show. Depending on the size of your group, you can present these via a TV, projector, or computer screen.
- Lay the newspapers down on the floor for students to pour soup onto, and keep paper towels close at hand for clean up.
- (optional) Have a clip of *The Prince of Egypt* cued to show the scene beginning in scene twenty-three at 73:00 (or, 1 hour, 13 minutes). You'll end the clip at 76:10 (or, 1 hour, 16 minutes, 10 seconds).

pit·tip

You can really spice up this activity with a real, live frog. You can often buy these inexpensively at pet stores (if you don't live in a location that is frog-infested). Bring the frog in a container to keep it safe. Remind students to be gentle as they touch the frog. Carefully pass the frog around the room so each student can hold it.

Make sure you keep the frog in a safe container, but keep it in sight of the group through the rest of the study.

The Goo...

Begin with the lights out or dimmed so that students won't be able to clearly see what's in the sealed bags. Do your best to imply that the bugs in the water are very, very real. You can also have a towel or cloth wrapped around the water-filled bags to further obscure the view.

SAY I've collected a few samples of local animal life, now sealed in formaldehyde. If you think you're up to it, go ahead and stick a finger in the bags to figure out what's in them.

➜ *Unseal the bags with great drama. Then, gingerly holding the bags, you and a couple volunteers should pass by the students. Slow down long enough for the braver students to stick a finger in the water (not knowing what's in it), but don't linger.*

Without revealing what was actually in the bags, discuss.

ASK
· What does it feel like to be close to critters like these?

· On a scale of one to ten, how much did you trust me during this activity?

· If you were to see a bug or frog on the ground somewhere, would you be inclined to pick it up? Why or why not?

· What are your biggest fears of the insect, reptile, natural-disaster, or just-plain-gross variety? How do you react to the very thought of it?

SAY Today we're going to look at a text in the Bible where the Egyptians got up close and personal with a wide variety of these kinds of things… and more.

ASK
· When do you ever think about God being in control of nature? What does that show you about how we can trust God?

· What do you already know about the story of the plagues? What questions do you have about the plagues?

SAY Let's try to answer those questions as we dig into this fascinating— and, let's be honest, pretty out-there—story. As we learn about the plagues that affected Egypt, we'll learn more about why we can have ultimate trust in God.

BELIEVE IT OR NOT

Talk about weird…and gross. A junior high teacher on a school field trip once discovered a pond full of hundreds of frogs, all of which had missing or deformed legs. Some of them had pairs of legs where there was only supposed to be one. Some had feet that were pointing in the wrong direction. Some had legs that wouldn't bend or that bent too much. Scientists still debate about whether it was caused by pesticides, parasites, or something else.

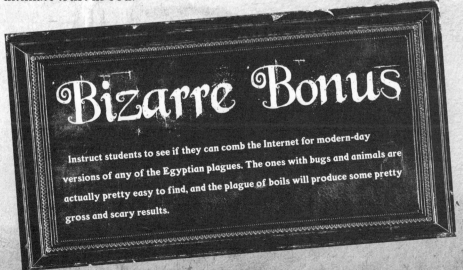

Bizarre Bonus

Instruct students to see if they can comb the Internet for modern-day versions of any of the Egyptian plagues. The ones with bugs and animals are actually pretty easy to find, and the plague of boils will produce some pretty gross and scary results.

You'll display (of course) ten images: a picture of the Nile river, a picture of a frog, a picture of a louse, a picture of a swarm of flies, a picture of a dead cow, a picture of boiling water, a picture of hail, a picture of a swarm of locusts, a picture of dark clouds, and a picture of a tombstone. Prepare these to be shown one at a time as you describe the plagues.

SAY Many of us grew up in Sunday school learning the cute stories of the Bible: Noah and the cute animals, Daniel and the cute lions, and so on. We may learn bits and pieces about the life of Moses along the way, but usually only in a G-rated kind of way.

ASK · What do you know about Moses off the top of your head? write on board

SAY Well, there is a dark side to the story of the Exodus. The ten plagues were not cute. How cute can lice be? Or imagine that you happen to be the poor soul going for a swim in the Nile the day it turned to blood? Can you say, "Everyone out of the pool?"

Moses told Pharaoh to let his people go. You don't want to say "No" to God's messenger. I want to show you what actually went on in Egypt way back when. This isn't the Sunday school-approved version, but here goes.

➔ *Show the images in turn as you talk about each plague.*

SAY The first was a plague of blood. The rivers literally turned to blood…can you imagine? Think for a moment about an entire river of blood—not just looking red. How would it look, smell, feel?

You would think that the tainting of the water that you depend on every day for drinking, washing, and bathing might change the mind of a dictator like the Pharaoh. But Pharaoh's magicians pulled out packages of Kool-Aid and dropped them in their own water, which, I guess, made the miracle look less impressive. Pharaoh wouldn't budge.

The second was a plague of frogs. A day after the Nile is turned to blood, the amphibians come crawling out, all over the city. This time Moses prayed that the plague would stop, and dead frogs were left in gigantic piles all over the countryside. But since the frogs were dead, Pharaoh wouldn't budge.

The third was a plague of lice (or gnats). Pharaoh's magicians couldn't do the same trick, and this time Pharaoh just chose to scratch — a lot — and wouldn't budge.

The fourth was a plague of flies. You know how bad it is when there's one fly circling your head. Well, picture swarming, buzzing, annoying, gross flies…everywhere. The plague came only to the Egyptian households, and finally Pharaoh caved. He told Moses to leave town for a few days to worship his God, but at the last minute, Pharaoh reneged, and wouldn't budge.

The fifth plague killed the livestock of the Egyptians. These animals were crucial to the people's livelihood, so this was an enormous loss. But, beyond that, envision what this looked like: the dead, bloated, rotted bodies of livestock scattered everywhere. There are probably too many dead animals to figure out what to do with them, since it's not like they could burn or bury them all in record-time. This was a truly awful, devastating blow. But still, amazingly, Pharaoh wouldn't budge.

The sixth plague was one of boils.

➡️ *Here is where you show the slide of boiling water, which is a little more tasteful than showing an image of a skin disease. Of course, if you want to…*

Moses threw a little dust in the air, and in a little while the entire population of Egyptians and animals broke out in skin sores. How creepy is this one — their bodies covered in painful, oozing boils. Gross! Still, Pharaoh would not budge.

The seventh was a plague of hail. We're talking hail like bullets, hail that even ripped the trees down. Bear in mind, these are people who live in the desert. These are people who were used to wearing headgear to keep the sun off of their necks all the time. On top of that, this was a few thousand years before refrigerators were invented. No one had even heard of ice falling from the sky that close to the equator. You have to have some concerns about whether or not your gods are mad at you when ice, which you've never seen, starts falling out of the sky, which never happens. Pharaoh must have been hit on the head by one of those chunks of ice, because still he wouldn't budge.

The eighth plague was one of locusts. What little of their crops that wasn't destroyed by the hail was eaten by the aggressive, loud, scary locusts. Pharaoh started to bargain with Moses about letting a few people go, but changed his mind after God swept the locusts away, and would not budge.

The ninth plague was a day of darkness. Not a single shred of light. Close your eyes to better imagine this. In a land of sun and deserts, this total darkness was not a good sign. The people already felt discouraged and terrified—this overwhelming darkness probably eliminated any leftover hope. And Pharaoh finally told Moses not to bother him with any more plagues, but still he wouldn't budge.

The 10th plague is one of the darkest points in the Bible. The Spirit of God passed through Egypt, actually killing the firstborn son of every household…except those that had smeared the blood of a lamb over their doorway. Now, think what it would be like if *every* household lost a child today. Can you picture just how terrible the desolation in Egypt was at this point? There was no food, no water, no livestock, many buildings were destroyed, everyone was sick with boils—and now every house was mourning the death of a child. This is worse than war in the awful level of terror and hopelessness and pain.

And yes…the Israelites were unharmed.

Finally Pharaoh's will was broken and the people fled.

ASK
- **What would it have felt like to be a poor Egyptian citizen living during these events?**
- **Why do you think Pharaoh refused to let the Israelites go?**
- **What kind of trust would Moses have to have had in order to follow God's commands? How did God prove to be trustworthy?**
- **Why do you think Jesus is sometimes called the "Lamb of God?" considering what you know about the tenth plague?**

· Does the story of the plagues raise questions for you about God?

· How does the story of the plagues affect or change the way you think about God? the way you might trust God? Explain.

Distribute the photocopied handout (p. 18) to every student in the room.

SAY In ancient Egypt, there was a whole pantheon of gods. There was a god of the sun, a god of the sea, a god of the rivers, and so on. It has been suggested that each of the plagues of Egypt is related to one of the gods of Egypt. For instance, the first plague, in which rivers turn to blood, would correspond to the Egyptian god of rivers. The fact that Moses could have power over the things that the Egyptian gods were supposed to have control over would be pretty embarrassing for those gods. Look at the sheets I've handed you to see what gods the plagues might correspond to.

 Have students form pairs.

SAY With your partner, think of at least five things that get in the way of people trusting God. Imagine each of these things as a god, and give that god a name. For instance, unhealthy dating relationships can distract us from trusting God to provide us with a good relationship—or the courage to be alone. So, we might say that the false god of dating relationships is called Cupid or Valentine. Think of five of them right now.

 Give them a few minutes to do so.

SAY Now imagine we're back in the days of Egypt. What kind of

"It [Egypt] has more wonders in it than any other country in the world and provides more works that defy description than any other place."
—Herodotus, Greek historian

15

plague might correspond to that false god? Would the false god Valentine be embarrassed by a plague of wilted flowers and stale chocolates? Think of a plague for each one.

 *Again, give them a few minutes for this.*

ASK · **What might God really do to free us from the things that distract us from completely trusting him?**

· **How are the false gods working the hardest to distract you from a personal relationship with Jesus?**

· **What can we do to avoid being distracted from trusting God by these things?**

 *Distribute fine tipped markers to the group.*

SAY Use your ten fingers to create ten things you want to remember in prayer. Pharaoh wouldn't listen despite God's many warnings. Perhaps we can remember God's goodness so we can be more open to trusting him.

The Gel...

On each finger, write one thing that makes you trust God. It might be a single word like "Jesus" or a phrase like "his protection" or "answered prayer." You can use the front or back of your fingers, as long as there is one on each.

 *Divide students into pairs and tell them to share what they wrote and why.*

pit·tip

Whenever dividing students into groups, be mindful of students who may get left out and take it personally. It's best to tell them when they split into pairs that "three is OK," so a stray person doesn't feel omitted. If you notice a regular habit of students pairing up with their close friends and ignoring newcomers, pull your more mature students aside and ask them to be conscious of people who are sometimes left out.

BEGIN CLEANING UP

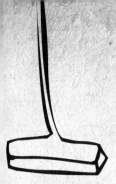

CLEANING UP

Here are some additional open-ended, thought-provoking questions. Use all or some of them to complement—or even replace—the debriefing questions for any of the activities in this study. You can guide students through this section all together or form smaller discussion groups for more intimate dialogue.

- **What makes it easy or difficult to trust God?**

- **What events might occur in your life to make it easier to trust God?**

- **How does it feel to trust someone and find out that they are, in fact, trustworthy?**

- **Why might God have had to use such extreme measures as the plagues to communicate his will?**

- **What effect did the plagues have on the Israelites who survived them and fled?**

- **After having witnessed the plagues, why do you think the Israelites would later complain to Moses for having led them into the desert? How does God's trustworthiness in the past help us trust him now and in the future?**

- **What biblical stories can you think of in which someone trusted God?**

- **Do you think God always provides justice for people who are oppressed? Why or why not?**

- **How might the story of the plagues still have the power to affect our faith today?**

- **How might our faith be different if we did not have the story of the plagues?**

Mixing It Up

Numbers 11:31-34
(another plague)

Mark 4:35-41
(proof that God controls nature)

Revelation 6
(a prophecy of coming wrath)

ONE GOD PER PLAGUE?

Here is a list of Egyptian gods that *may* have corresponded to the plagues, suggesting that God was intentionally showing Pharaoh that his gods had no power.

The rivers of blood	Hapi (the god of the Nile)
Frogs	Heqt (a fertility goddess who appeared as a frog)
Lice	Kheper (god of beetles and flies)
Flies	Kheper
Livestock	Apis (the sacred bull)
Boils	Imhotep (physician god)
Hail	Nut (goddess of the sky)
Locusts	Seth (god of crops)
Darkness	Ra (the sun god)
First born	Pharaoh

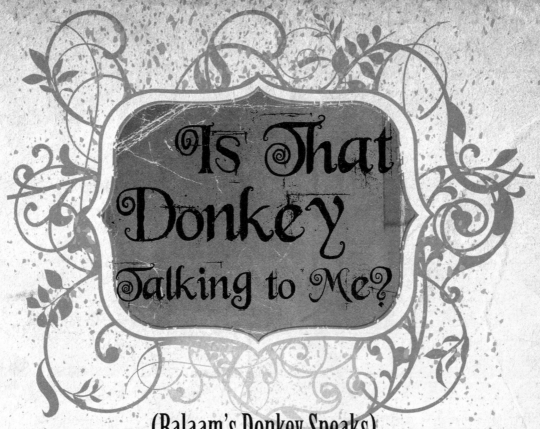

Is That Donkey Talking to Me?

(Balaam's Donkey Speaks)

BIBLE STORY: NUMBERS 22:1-41

THEME: GOD'S GUIDANCE (THROUGH SURPRISING MESSENGERS)
Subtopics: God's Will, Patience, Listening to God, Stress

Students will explore the story of Balaam, whose donkey God uses to guide Balaam to humility and obedience. Students will learn to recognize and listen to God's unlikely messengers in their life, while surrendering the roadblocks that stand in the way.

SUPPLIES NEEDED:
- a piece of notebook or printer paper for each student
- pens
- containers of mustard, mayonnaise, hand lotion, Pepto Bismol, sand, (and any other unlikely but everyday substances)
- toothpicks
- at least 12 three-inch pieces of string or yarn
- sheets or pieces of plastic (tarp)
- paper towels
- (optional) CD player
- (optional) Sonicflood album *Sonicflood*
- Bibles

PREPARATION AND SETUP:

- Make copies of "Unlikely Messengers" handout (p. 29) for every student.

- (optional) Have the CD player cued to the song "Open the Eyes of My Heart" from the album *Sonicflood*.

BELIEVE IT OR NOT

In Balaam's story, God utilizes a donkey as an unlikely messenger of wisdom. Consider this story where a pigeon and a dog became unlikely war heroes during World War II.

Over 50 years ago, Tyke, a Cairo-born pigeon and Peter, a British collie dog, were awarded two Dickin medals, the equivalent of the Victoria Cross, for their brave service during the war. Peter was responsible for saving the lives of six people buried under rubble during the Blitz, and Tyke carried a message over 100 miles, which resulted in the rescue of an entire air crew. Believe it or not, God uses unlikely messengers to bring us wisdom and hope, and in the case of Tyke and Peter—life.

SAY Think for a moment about the most important thing you've ever learned in your life. It could be anything, about anything, and have been taught to you by anyone. Keep that thing you learned in mind while I give you some items.

→ *Have students form groups of three or four, and give each group a collection of offbeat but everyday items: mustard, mayonnaise, hand lotion, Pepto Bismol, sand, toothpicks, pieces of string or yarn, and so on. Make sure this is all students have, and that they do not have access to pens, markers, and so on. You may choose to give each student a piece of paper, but you might also encourage more creativity by leaving them with only the minimal materials. However, to protect the floor, set down sheets or a tarp where the students will be working.*

SAY Now, your mission over the next three minutes is to express the most important thing you've ever learned…using only the items I've given you. Be resourceful and innovative—and feel free to share ideas with each other. After three minutes, each of you will share your creation with the group.

→ *Let the students get to work expressing their biggest lesson with the unusual materials; they might draw a picture, try to write something, or come up with a completely different approach. After three minutes, discuss.*

ASK
· What was this activity like for you? How was it surprising or difficult?

· How is this experience like or unlike actually learning something in real life?

· What kinds of similarities are there in the things you've all learned? What are the differences?

· You've shared the most important things you've ever learned, but please tell: when have you followed what you learned from that lesson? When haven't you? Explain.

SAY You just shared something in a very unusual, surprising way. But that's nothing compared to the unusual and surprising message God sent Balaam. Let's check it out.

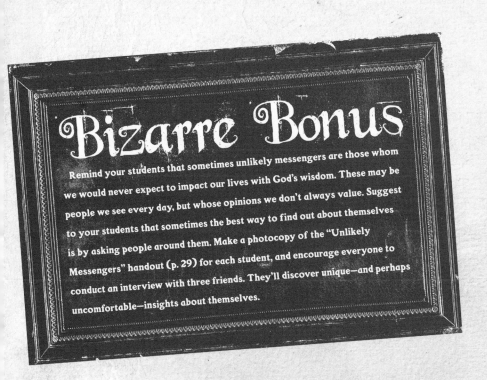

Bizarre Bonus

Remind your students that sometimes unlikely messengers are those whom we would never expect to impact our lives with God's wisdom. These may be people we see every day, but whose opinions we don't always value. Suggest to your students that sometimes the best way to find out about themselves is by asking people around them. Make a photocopy of the "Unlikely Messengers" handout (p. 29) for each student, and encourage everyone to conduct an interview with three friends. They'll discover unique—and perhaps uncomfortable—insights about themselves.

You'll need at least three volunteers to act out the characters in Numbers 22:21-34: Balaam, his donkey, and the angel. If you have a large group, have students form two or more sub-groups and ask for multiple volunteers. This way, you will be guiding several sets of the characters simultaneously.

You'll read the passage, and the volunteers will (silently) act out what you say (of course, remind students that Balaam's beatings should not be authentic; this is miming territory only).

SAY The story of Balaam's stubborn donkey uses the concept of road-blocks to illuminate the concept of hearing God's message and following him instead of pursuing our own way. Sometimes, God uses unexpected tools to communicate with us.

SAY For our Balaam, donkey, and angel actors: Your job is to act your parts as I read the passage.

SAY TO AUDIENCE

As the chapter is acted out, note the effect the roadblock has on both Balaam and his donkey.

Balaam is asked by King Balak to curse the Israelites so he will be victorious in battle. God tells Balaam that he should not go with King Balak. However, Balaam asks God a second time, and this time, God instructs him to go. This is where our story begins:

So the next morning Balaam got up, saddled his nice little donkey, and headed toward King Balak.

But God wanted to send Balaam a message, so he sent an angel to block the road. As Balaam was riding along, his donkey saw the angel standing in the road...with a drawn sword in his hand! The poor freaked-out donkey probably wondered why Balaam kept prodding him on, what with this angel in front of them, and ran off the road.

But Balaam couldn't see the angel, so he decided on this brilliant idea: beat the donkey and continue on. This time, the angel made things a little tougher, standing at a narrow spot between two walls. The poor stressed donkey tried to squeeze by the angel...and accidentally crushed Balaam's foot. So, what did Balaam do? You guessed it: again he hit his faithful donkey.

Then the angel moved farther down the road and stood in a place way too narrow for the donkey to get by. This time, the donkey had had enough—it gave up and just laid down. Predictably, Balaam beat his donkey for the *third* time.

Then God did something amazing: the donkey turned to Balaam and spoke to him: "What's wrong with you? Three beatings? Is this really necessary?"

Without the smallest shock, Balaam responded arrogantly, "You've made me look like a fool! If I had a sword, I'd kill you!"

"But it's me, your favorite donkey! Think about it, Balaam. Have I ever done anything like this before?"

"No," Balaam admitted, as he scuffed his sandal in the dust.

Then God opened Balaam's eyes, and he saw the angel. Immediately, Balaam bowed his head and fell face down on the ground. Talk about embarrassing…

"Why did you beat your donkey three times in a row?" the angel asked. When Balaam didn't respond, the angel said, "Look, I've blocked your way because you're stubbornly resisting God's will. Come on, Balaam! Even your donkey knows how to show proper respect!"

Then Balaam cried out his confession to the angel, and said: "I'm sorry. I've sinned. I didn't realize you were standing in the road to block my way. I'll go back home if you don't want me to go."

But the angel replied, a bit more softly, "Go to King Balak, but only say what God tells you to say, all right?"

 Have students sit down to discuss the story.

> **MEDIA INFUSION (optional)**
> Play the song "Open the Eyes of My Heart, Lord" by Sonicflood from the album *Sonicflood*. Afterward, discuss.
> **ASK •** How does this song reveal what Balaam must have felt after he was scolded by both his donkey and an angel of the Lord in the space of five minutes?
> **•** When was a time God got your attention in a dramatic way? What happened?

ASK
· What was it like to watch the story unfold in this way?

· What words would you use to describe Balaam at the beginning of the story? the middle? the very end?

· Why do you think God chose to use the donkey, of all things, to send a message to Balaam?

· What might it reveal about God that he uses such surprising methods to guide his people?

SAY Balaam's story shows us pretty clearly that when we keep going our way, ignoring God's message or redirection, we really only make things worse. God uses whatever means are necessary to bring us to our senses and deliver the message we need to hear, so we will closely follow him.

SAY The angel God sent was the technical roadblock…yet the actual roadblocks in Balaam's path were his pride and arrogance. These were preventing him from hearing and obeying God's message. It's not always easy to recognize roadblocks to God's messages. I mean, Balaam, this big-time prophet, chose to believe his faithful donkey was just randomly acting stupid…but really, God was trying to communicate with him. Balaam beat his donkey three times before he realized that an angel of the Lord was blocking his path.

ASK · When have you not seen God communicating with you? What kept you from hearing God's message?

→ *Prompt students to think further about times when they felt God's guidance or intervention in their lives. These may be events such as: deaths, starting a new school, break-ups, fights with family, and so on.*

SAY Pair up with the person next to you and share about a time that you experienced God's presence in your life, although you couldn't physically prove it. How did God guide you in this situation? What type of messenger did he use?

→ *Have pairs continue discussing. Pause after each of these questions so students can answer with their partners.*

ASK · What roadblocks have you caused or encountered in the past? How did God redirect you, and help you hear his message?

· What roadblock might exist in your relationship with God right now? What's keeping you from hearing what God wants to tell you? What evidence do you see of this?

· What reasons might God have for using dramatic or surprising messengers to reveal his guidance?

· Rather than just having you obey for the sake of obeying, what are God's purposes in guiding you?

➜ *Have students stand up and form one large circle. Give everybody a piece of paper and a pen.*

SAY You just learned a lot about someone else's life—their past experiences, current fears and goals, views on God, and more. You talked a lot about how God uses surprising messengers in your lives. Now, I'd like you to give each other a message of affirmation. Spend a minute writing down something you think your partner needs to know or hear… perhaps an encouragement to keep obeying God, a relevant Scripture verse, or something else. Basically, write down what you think God wants your friend to know so that he or she will draw closer to Jesus. But, and this is really important, first make sure to write your partner's name very clearly at the top of the paper.

➜ *Wait for students to finish writing their messages. Remind them again to make sure their friend's name is at the top of the message.*

SAY Now, considering where we are, you may not be the most surprising messenger of God. However, the way we're delivering these messages will be a bit surprising.

Have students crumple up their messages into paper balls, then have everybody close their eyes, and, on your count of three, all throw the messages into the middle of the circle.

Then tell students to open their eyes and try to find their own message.

 After everyone has received and read their message, continue.

SAY Let's take a few moments to connect with God about where and how he's guiding us individually. Even though it takes Balaam three tries to recognize God's presence on the road (with the help of his donkey), he eventually admits his error and humbly asks for God's forgiveness. His confession is comprised of three simple sentences:

"I have sinned."

"I didn't realize you sent an angel to block my way."

"I will go back home if you want me to."

The first sentence represents Balaam's confession. The second sentence reflects his humility. And the third sentence reveals his submission to God's will. Take a moment to think about an area of your life where God is redirecting you. What pops into your head may be kind of a surprise, but that's exactly what we're talking about: the unexpected messengers and methods God uses to guide us closer to him.

Reflect for a moment on how God might want to redirect you or what message God might want to send you. This might be a good kind of redirection, or it might require your repentance. Either way, think about what impact your obedience and humility will have—especially on your relationship with Jesus. Then, prepare to surrender this to God and ask him to draw you in a new direction.

 In a time of prayer, over the next five or six minutes, ask students to follow Balaam's example: offer confession (if necessary), then humility, and finally submission to God's redirection.

The Gel...

Over the next several weeks, plan to begin each prayer time by committing to follow this new direction—or any others God reveals to you. Ask God to illuminate where you're not hearing his communication and clearly show you his message. As the weeks progress, I suggest you map out your progress in a prayer journal: how you are maturing in your decision-making, in what ways are you growing closer to Jesus, and so on.

pit·tip

Remind students that unlikely messengers could be people they talk to every day or people from whom they won't expect to receive God's wisdom. This will be a difficult concept for some students. They will struggle to understand that, because God desires to connect with us, he may choose to employ different tactics in order to commune with us on a personal level. Encourage them to remember the lesson of Balaam, and not to overlook the "donkeys" in their lives.

BEGIN CLEANING UP

CLEANING UP

Here are some additional open-ended, thought-provoking questions. Use all or some of them to complement—or even replace—the debriefing questions for any of the activities in this study. You can guide students through this section all together or form smaller discussion groups for more intimate dialogue.

· **Why do you think Balaam asks God twice if he should go to King Balak?**

"We are either in the process of resisting God's truth or in the process of being shaped and molded by his truth."3
—Charles Stanley

- Why is God angry with Balaam for going to King Balak after he instructs to do so (v. 22)?

- Balaam seems to speak easily to his donkey, without registering any shock. Why do you think this is?

- What does Balaam's reaction to the angel show you about his relationship with God?

- Who is the donkey in your life—the person who has called your attention to God's direction for your life?

- How do you react when you encounter a roadblock to receiving God's message (such as difficulty praying or not reading the Bible)?

- Give an example of an area where you're not necessarily sinning (like Balaam), but where God is still redirecting you. How will you respond?

- In your relationship with Jesus, are you quick to ask forgiveness? Or do you hold onto your mistakes and pretend he doesn't know? Explain.

Mixing It Up

Luke 42: 54-62
(Peter's denial of Christ)

Luke 1: 26-38
(Mary and the angel)

Jonah 1: 1-17
(Jonah runs away from God)

UNLIKELY MESSENGERS

Are you really open to letting an unlikely messenger affect your life with God's wisdom? Are you sure? Sometimes the best way to find out about yourself is by asking those around you. Use this handout to interview your three closest friends, family members, and so on. They must be honest in their answers! You may be surprised at how others see you.

In what ways do you see me believing in the unexpected or surprising, especially when it comes to faith?

If you blindfolded me and told me to eat what felt like a bowl of worms, what would I do?

I want to be someone who learns well, especially when God wants to change my path. Can you give an example of how I've done this?

How well do I handle confrontation? Explain.

What three words would you use to describe the kind of friend I am?

When life is hard, I react to the challenge by...
Three ways I really reflect God's presence in my life are:

How would you describe the way I think of or feel about Jesus?

What message do you think God might want to give me at this point in my life? What should I do about it?

Hair-Raising (and Head-Splitting) Courage

(Jael Drives Tent Peg Through Enemy Soldier's Head)

BIBLE STORY: JUDGES 4:1-23

❦ ∼

THEME: COURAGE WHEN IT COUNTS

Subtopics: Leadership, God's Acts, Following God, Rescue

Students will test their courage, examine Jael's tremendous example of courage, and commit to depending on God for courage.

SUPPLIES NEEDED:
- index cards
- pens
- at least two mystery foods for each group (see note)
- a bucket of ice water for each group
- a blown-up balloon
- Bibles
- safety pin
- blanket
- two squirt bottles of water
- paper
- a sheet of newsprint or a white board
- marker
- (optional) TV, DVD player, and the movie *Finding Nemo*

A note on mystery foods: You know your group and what you can and can't get away with (and what you can and can't afford). Given your own parameters, choose your mystery foods so they will require courage but won't tip the scales unnecessarily. You can choose something like a jar of baby food, a pureed Happy Meal, or even a candy bar—since students won't know what it is in advance, even a treat can require a courageous step forward (so long as other groups don't get wind of it!).

PREPARATION AND SETUP:

- Prepare one set of "Courage Cards" for every six students you anticipate. Label index cards in sets of five as follows: Sing "I'm a Little Teacup" and do the motions; Eat a mystery food; Hold your hand in a bucket of ice water for 30 seconds; Honestly answer one clean question from another group member; Do an all-out loud-and-crazy victory dance/cheer for 30 seconds.
- Make at least six copies of the script handout (pp. 39-40): for yourself (to follow along), the Narrator, Sisera, Deborah, Barak, and Jael.
- Make three signs: "Lord, help us!", "Battle Cry!", and "Panic Cry!" These will be used by the actors during the drama.

- Put essential skit supplies out of sight, with the balloon under the blanket, the safety pin in an easy-to-grab pocket so you can slip it to the actor who plays Sisera, and squirt bottles hidden where you'll be able to easily reach them when needed.
- Gather any other props you want to use during the drama. Costumes, plastic or foam swords and shields, a blanket, a cup, and a hammer and tent stake will all add to the overall effect of the script.
- (optional) Set up the TV and DVD player, and cue *Finding Nemo* to chapter 21, where the counter reads 1:08:08 and Marlin and Dory are inside the whale. You'll stop the scene at 1:13:48.

Ask students to form groups of six, sit in a circle, and choose a leader.

SAY I will give each group leader a set of Courage Cards. Each card has an action written on it that you might perform, if you have the courage. Your leader will silently read the cards and decide who to assign each task to. Once the leader has decided who to assign an action to, he or she will place it action-side down in front of that person. When your leader has assigned an action to each group member, you may silently read your card. Your group will then take a silent vote. If you hold up one finger you are saying, yes, you have the courage to perform that action. If you hold up two fingers you are saying, no, I don't want to do the task, and I want to challenge our leader's courage.

If the majority of your group votes yes, everyone will perform their task and your leader, by nature of their good leadership, won't perform any action. Those in the minority—who voted no—will be forced to perform

If you have less than six students or your group doesn't divide easily by six, give each group one less card than the number of students; a group of six gets five cards, so a group of five gets four cards, and so on.

their task plus the task of the person seated on their left.

If the majority of your group votes no, all cards will be collected, passed to the person to the leader's right—who is the new group leader—and play begins again.

If a new leader needs to take charge, when tasks are performed, the former leader will perform two tasks of the new leader's choosing. Your group can only pass leadership to a new leader twice, so play carefully.

Leaders, assign Courage Cards carefully—as this is a call to courage, you don't want to give tasks to people who will perform them too easily. However, you don't want to assign them to people you know won't do them—and thus end up performing more tasks yourself.

→ *Allow time for groups to play. When everyone has performed their tasks,*

ASK · What risk did you face as you prepared to cast your vote?

· How did you feel as you performed your task?

· If you could do it all again would you vote differently?

Why or why not?

· What kind of courage did this game require?

SAY As you might have guessed, today's topic is "Courage When It Counts." And, while you needed some courage to play our game, courage can be deadly serious. Today we'll look at a Bible story from Judges 4 to see how one woman used her head and displayed tremendous courage to take off someone else's head.

BELIEVE IT OR NOT
Against all odds, a construction worker from Los Angeles, California, survived after slipping and accidentally firing six nails from his nail gun into his head and spinal column. In May 2004, 39-year-old Isidro Mejia was rushed to the hospital, where it took surgeons five days to remove the six nails, four of which were embedded in his skull and another lodged in his spinal column. While the operating neurosurgeon said that his injuries ought to have ended his life, Mejia was expected to make a full recovery.

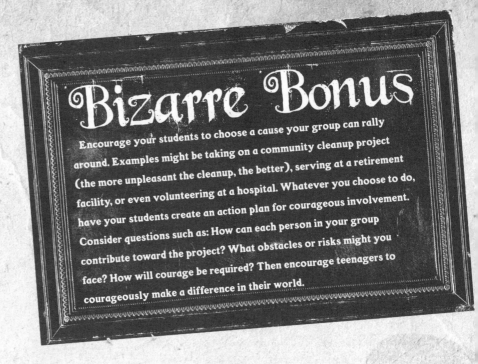

Bizarre Bonus

Encourage your students to choose a cause your group can rally around. Examples might be taking on a community cleanup project (the more unpleasant the cleanup, the better), serving at a retirement facility, or even volunteering at a hospital. Whatever you choose to do, have your students create an action plan for courageous involvement. Consider questions such as: How can each person in your group contribute toward the project? What obstacles or risks might you face? How will courage be required? Then encourage teenagers to courageously make a difference in their world.

The Guts...

You'll need volunteers to read/act the following parts: Narrator, Sisera, Deborah, Barak, and Jael. Distribute a copy of the script (pp. 39-40) to each actor, and set out the three signs so the appropriate actor can use them at the right times to spark the needed response.

Ask your group to sit in a circle, leaving space for your actors to sit together. Meanwhile, have a little chat with your actors: tell them that when the narrator reads that Jael pounds a peg through Sisera's head, Sisera will be under a blanket and can pop a balloon (slip Sisera the pin to put in a pocket now!). At the same time, you and the narrator will grab squirt bottles of water and squirt the group. Jael and Sisera will need to keep the balloon concealed as they cover him with the blanket.

➡️ *Ask actors to join the circle and stand when they act out their parts. When the drama is over, have students return to their small groups as you distribute Bibles, pen, and paper.*

pit·tip

If you have more students than can comfortably sit in a circle, at least have students sit close together so there is space around the group in which actors can run.

SAY Reread the story from Judges 4 and make a list of all the courageous acts you see people involved in. For each act of courage you find, imagine what that might look like in your world. For example, for me, Jael stabbing Sisera with the tent peg looks like telling a friend how they've hurt me. Once you've got your list, read Joshua 1:9 and Psalm 31:23-24 and discuss this question:

- **What do these verses tell us about courage?**

➡️ *Give groups a few minutes to work, then ask each group to share one or two examples of courage, both from the story and in today's world.*

ASK · Why is courage important?

· How can the Bible passages we've looked at today help us to have courage when it counts?

SAY Courage means different things to different people. For one person, speaking in front of a group requires massive courage, while for another it's as natural as can be. One person needs courage to ride a Ferris wheel, while another enjoys rock climbing as high as they can go. But all of us need courage in small and large doses, and God will be the source of courage when it counts, if we let him. We won't all be heroes like Jael, knocking out the enemy of the nation, but we need courage to do what God requires of each one of us.

BELIEVE IT OR NOT

It doesn't sound like the breakfast of champions, but beans on toast may be your best breakfast bet for boosting brainpower. Studies have shown that what you eat definitely affects how well you think. For example, not eating breakfast negatively impacts how well you do in school. But students who ate toast scored high on a series of tests, and those who ate beans on toast scored higher still. Those whose breakfasts included sugary drinks and foods performed about as well as the average 70-year-old. Of course, having brains enough to avoid having your brains bashed during someone else's courageous act goes far toward doing well in school and life!

 **The Grit...** **Direct students to the newsprint.**

SAY So let's come up with a list of courage-required situations for people your age.

➡ *(Write any that students have already suggested in "The Goo..." activity.)*

This list could include things like: leaving home for the first time, standing up for what you know is right, trying new things, following your dreams, sharing about Jesus with others, obeying God, or making new friends.

ASK · **How do you feel as you look at this list?**

Is it energizing, scary, overwhelming, exciting, that's life...?

· **Think for a moment about your spiritual faith and relationship with Jesus—no matter how close or not close it is. Now, consider: what courage might be necessary when it comes to exploring this relationship? growing in this relationship?**

· **In what ways have you discovered that good risks tend to lead to the best results? Why might God prefer we live with courage?**

· **How can friends or family members help us have courage?**

MEDIA INFUSION (optional)
ASK • When have you needed courage?
SAY We're going to watch a movie clip to see an example of someone who needs courage to trust a friend who is trying to save their lives. Show chapter 21 (1:08:06 to 1:13:48) of *Finding Nemo* with Marlin and Dory inside the whale.
ASK • Why was it so hard for Marlin to trust Dory? to let go?
• How is this scene similar to Barak needing to trust Deborah? How is it different?
• Who had greater courage: Marlin or Barak? Why?

SAY The word *encourage* really means to give someone courage. Let's practice that right now.

➡ *Have students turn to a partner and say at least two nice things about them that might give them courage this week. For example, they might share how they noticed their partner doing something nice for someone or how impressed they were with their answer in history class.*

The Gel...

SAY Prayer is another way we can encourage each other. Take another look at our list as you think about situations in your life this next week and month that will require you to act with courage. Share with your partner one courage-required situation you expect to face, and pray for each other to be strong and courageous.

➡ *Challenge students to commit to pray for their partner each day this week.*

BEGIN CLEANING UP

> "What makes a king out of a slave! ...Courage! What makes the flag on the mast to wave! ...Courage! ...What makes the sphinx the seventh wonder? ...Courage! What makes the dawn come up like thunder? ...Courage! ...What have they got that I ain't got? Courage!"
>
> —Cowardly Lion,
> *The Wizard of Oz* (1939)

CLEANING UP

Here are some additional open-ended, thought-provoking questions. Use all or some of them to complement—or even replace—the debriefing questions for any of the activities in this study. You can guide students through this section all together or form smaller discussion groups for more intimate dialogue.

- Why do you think Barak wanted Deborah to accompany him into battle? Why do you think Scripture indicates that this was not the best choice?

- What was God's role in the battle? What was Barak's role? What does that tell you about human accomplishments?

- Which character in Judges 4 do you most identify with? Why?

- Judges 5 records a song Deborah and Barak sang to God about this story. Read Judges 5:2, 24-27. How did Jael display cunning and courage?

- According to Judges 4:1, how could the Israelites have avoided this whole situation? Why is that meaningful?

- What has God done for you? How has this increased your level of courage for the future?

- How can remembering what God has done for you make a difference in your life? Draw you closer to Jesus?

- Joshua 1:9 says do not be afraid or discouraged. What discourages or scares people your age?

- How does Jesus' great act of courage in dying for our sins inspire you?

- How can you remember to rely on God for courage?

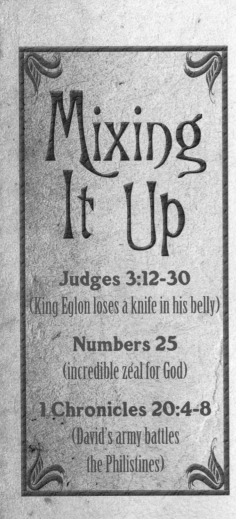

Mixing It Up

Judges 3:12-30
(King Eglon loses a knife in his belly)

Numbers 25
(incredible zeal for God)

1 Chronicles 20:4-8
(David's army battles the Philistines)

DRAMA SCRIPT

NARRATOR: THE ISRAELITES QUICKLY FORGOT ALL THAT GOD HAD DONE FOR THEM, AND THEY DID WHAT WAS EVIL IN THE LORD'S SIGHT. SO THE LORD HANDED THEM OVER TO KING JABIN THE CANAANITE.

Sisera: I am Sisera, commander of King Jabin's army. I have 900 iron chariots, and I ruthlessly oppressed the Israelites for 20 years.

NARRATOR: THEN THE ISRAELITES CRIED OUT TO THE LORD FOR HELP.

Israelites: Lord, help us!

Deborah: I am Deborah, a prophet who became a judge in Israel. I hold court under the Palm of Deborah, and the Israelites come to me to settle their disputes.

NARRATOR: ONE DAY DEBORAH SENT FOR A GUY NAMED BARAK.

Deborah: The Lord, the God of Israel, commands you: "Assemble 10,000 warriors at Mount Tabor. I will lure Sisera, along with his chariots and warriors, to the Kishon River. There I will give you victory over him."

Barak: I will go, but only if you go with me!

Deborah: I will go. But since you have made this choice, you will receive no honor. The Lord's victory over Sisera will be at the hands of a woman.

NARRATOR: SO BARAK, 10,000 WARRIORS, AND DEBORAH MARCHED AGAINST THE CANAANITES.

(Barak & Deborah march around the group.)

Sisera: When I heard that Barak was coming against me, I called all 900 of my iron chariots and all of my warriors together.

NARRATOR: AND JUST SO YOU KNOW, AN ISRAELITE NAMED HEBER THE KENITE, A DESCENDANT OF MOSES' BROTHER-IN-LAW, HAD PITCHED HIS TENT AWAY FROM THE OTHER MEMBERS OF HIS TRIBE, NEAR WHERE THE ISRAELITES ARMY WAS GATHERING. HANG ONTO THAT INFO FOR A BIT...

Deborah *(to Barak)***:** Get ready! Today the LORD will give you victory over Sisera, for the LORD is marching ahead of you.

NARRATOR: SO BARAK LED HIS 10,000 WARRIORS INTO BATTLE.

(Barak leads everyone in a loud, wild battle cry.)

Barak: When we attacked, the Lord threw Sisera and all his charioteers and warriors into a panic.

(Sisera leads everyone in a panicky cry.)

Sisera: I leaped down from my chariot and escaped on foot. *(Run around the group.)*

Barak: I chased the enemy and killed all of Sisera's warriors. *(Run around the group.)* Not a single one was left alive.

NARRATOR: MEANWHILE, SISERA RAN TO THE TENT *[Sisera runs around the group]* OF HEBER THE KENITE (REMEMBER HIM?), BECAUSE HEBER'S FAMILY WAS FRIENDLY WITH KING JABIN AND SISERA WAS LOOKING FOR A FRIENDLY FACE. HEBER WASN'T HOME, BUT HIS WIFE, JAEL WAS IN THE TENT.

Jael: I went out to meet Sisera. Come into my tent, sir. Come in. Don't be afraid.

NARRATOR: SO HE WENT INTO HER TENT, AND SHE COVERED HIM WITH A BLANKET.

Sisera: Please give me some water. I'm thirsty.

Jael: I gave him some milk and covered him again.

Sisera: Stand at the door of the tent. If anybody asks, say no one's here.

Jael: But Sisera was exhausted and fell asleep.

NARRATOR: BUT JAEL WAS NOT A FRIENDLY FACE...SHE WAS NOT ON KING JABIN'S OR SISERA'S SIDE. SHE WAS ON THE ISRAELITES' SIDE. ON GOD'S SIDE. SO JAEL QUIETLY CREPT UP TO HIM WITH A HAMMER AND TENT PEG. THEN SHE DROVE THE TENT PEG THROUGH HIS TEMPLE AND INTO THE GROUND.

[Pause for effects.]

Jael: And Sisera died.

NARRATOR: WHEN BARAK CAME LOOKING FOR SISERA...

Jael: ...I went out to meet him. Come, and I will show you the man you are hunting.

Barak: I followed Jael into the tent and found Sisera lying there dead, with the tent peg through his temple.

NARRATOR: SO ON THAT DAY, GOD HELPED A WOMAN DESTROY THE MIGHTY LEADER SISERA, AND ISRAEL SAW GOD SUBDUE JABIN, THE CANAANITE KING. AND FROM THAT TIME ON ISRAEL BECAME STRONGER AND STRONGER AGAINST KING JABIN, UNTIL THEY FINALLY DESTROYED HIM.

God vs. the gods

(Elijah Faces the Prophets of Baal)

BIBLE STORY: 1 KINGS 18:16-40

THEME: ONE TRUE GOD

Subtopics: Obedience, Faith, Power, Respect, God's Sovereignty, World Religions

Students will study the story of Elijah and the false prophets of Baal and then acknowledge that there is only one God who is worthy of worship and devotion.

SUPPLIES NEEDED:
- pens
- three sheets of balled-up newspaper
- a large cooking pot with a lid
- rubbing alcohol
- water
- three water bottles
- matches

- Bibles
- a prop bag (filled with a rubber insect, a stuffed animal, a small cardboard box, and lipstick, or other props you substitute)
- an index card for every student
- empty coffee can
- (optional) a TV/DVD player and a copy of *The Empire Strikes Back*

PREPARATION AND SETUP:

- Make a copy of the handout (p. 49) for every student.
- Prepare the metal cooking pot with three balled-up sheets of newspaper inside. Also make sure you have two bottles full of water, and a third bottle filled with rubbing alcohol.

- Prepare a bag of props using the four suggestions in the supply list or another collection of at least four items.
- (optional) Cue *The Empire Strikes Back* to 1:09:00, when Luke Skywalker says, "We'll never get it out now." You'll stop the scene at 1:12:50, after Yoda lifts the X-Wing out of the swamp.

BELIEVE IT OR NOT

Who knew something so small could be so, well…explosive? Pistachio nuts have been known to spontaneously combust when stored in large quantities, due to their high percentage of oil.

The Goo…

Divide the students into groups of four. Everyone needs the photocopied handout (p. 49) and a pen.

SAY In your group, I want you to each pick a major world religion. Don't tell the people in the group which one you are thinking of. Using your paper, write down different facts about that religion that you know or can think of. Don't worry too much about accuracy, because you're not going to be graded on this.

If you don't know much about one major religion, just think about what you know of several religions. Most importantly, be sure to include anything that you can think of that is gross or weird, like the important details of animal sacrifices, what kinds of punishments people suffer if they disobey it, beliefs about alien beings, body piercings, and so on.

 Give them a few minutes for this, then have them share with their groups what they've come up with.

ASK · **What were strangest or scariest parts of the religions you discussed?**

· **How would you feel about a belief system if you suspected someone else had made it up?**

· **How valid or complete are religions that we come up with on our own? Explain.**

· **What is different about the gods we invent and the real God?**

· **What do you think Jesus thinks about other religions?**

How does he feel about the people who practice them?

Explain your answer.

SAY Today we're going to look at the interaction between the one true God and the false gods that were worshipped in the ancient world.

Bizarre Bonus

Tell your students that the best way to get a feel for burnt offerings is to go home and practice on their own. Instruct them to go home and read the first chapter of Leviticus. Suggest they use a can of Spam to make a lamb, then show their parents how the sacrifice was performed by the high priest. However, remember: it's best not to encourage them to play with fire. Spam takes a while to cook anyway…

The Guts… To illustrate this story, you'll need some balled-up newspaper (about three sheets) and three water bottles: two filled with water, the third with rubbing alcohol. Place the rolled-up paper inside a large, metal cooking pot. Make sure you have a lid that fits over the pot.

SAY You know you're a complete punk when you show up to town and the first thing people ask you is what trouble you're there to cause. That's the kind of greeting the prophets tended to get, and Elijah was the biggest among them.

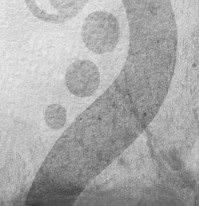

pit·tip

Talking about other religions is delicate but important. As the leader, you can model a respectful kind of disagreement with belief systems that are held by millions of people. Avoid name-calling or simplistic branding—when discussing other religions, try to present the other faiths in the most clear and accurate terms. Don't criticize minor issues or issues that might be culturally true of some of a religion's followers but not all (like a dress code). When you point out differences between Christianity and another faith, try to stick to the direct teachings of the Scriptures and their importance for our lives, observing the key ideas of other faiths that are different from the Bible. In the end, Elijah and the biblical witness will be a challenging enough critique that we don't have to add to its force.

So when God had a problem with Israel, he'd send Elijah in to stir things up. Nice job description, right?

When Ahab was king over Israel, he led the people to worship the false god Baal (which you can pronounce like "bail out the water" or like "a rubber ball"), which didn't exactly put him on God's Christmas list. So in comes Elijah, God's deputy.

Elijah's first command: "Bring me the 450 priests of this false god you've been worshiping and another 400 priests of another false god." I know what you're thinking: chili cook-off. But no, Elijah wanted to see whether or not Baal had the same power as his God. So he came up with a test.

"Build an altar," he said, "and then pray to your gods to make it burst into flames." Great idea, right, because who can do that? But picture 850 guys dancing around this altar from dawn to dusk expecting it to spontaneously combust at any moment. And on top of that, they had some pretty gross rituals to go along with their dancing, cutting themselves with swords to offer their own blood to their gods.

Now, as if it wasn't bad enough that they're dancing around an altar that's about as likely to burst into flame as a snowman, Elijah decides to have some fun with them. He actually comes out with, "You'll have to shout louder...perhaps he's on a trip or in the bathroom." You can see why the prophets often got killed.

Well, then it was Elijah's turn. He made an altar too. Just to make sure that everyone knew it would be completely impossible for his altar to catch fire, he poured water on it three different times.

→ *Have your group stand a few steps away for this illustration. Take the bottles of water and pour them around the base of the pile of newspapers. Try not to pour it directly over the top, but only around the base. With the third bottle, pour the rubbing alcohol directly over the newspapers, so that it looks like you are drenching them with water.*

SAY Then Elijah took a minute to pray to God, and poof!

→ *Drop a match onto the newspapers where you've poured the alcohol, and they should catch fire. After a few seconds, cover the pot with the lid to extinguish the fire.*

pit·tip

Whenever you think it's appropriate (probably after the re-enactment), make it clear that this isn't actually a miracle: let students know that you're actually using alcohol and not just water.

SAY Well, after that, the story didn't end too well for the false prophets.

ASK · So what are your initial reactions to the story?

· Why do you think Elijah went through this long ritual to make his point?

· What does this teach us about faith? about God?

· Why do you think God would care which god we believe in?

· How do you think Jesus wants us to react to other ideas about who he is?

→ *Ask the students to break into groups of four and read 1 Kings 11:1-11.*

ASK · How did Solomon fail? Why do you think he did so?

· In what ways are we are tempted to do the same thing in the modern world? Why?

The Grit... For this activity, you'll need four props in front of the room: a rubber insect, a stuffed animal, a cardboard box, and lipstick. Feel free to add other props for broader variety. The more you include, the easier and more creative the activity will be.

SAY You may or may not realize that a lot of the ancient religions required some bizarre rituals and sacrifices in order to honor their gods. Sometimes they burned incense. Other times they sacrificed animals. We're going to do a little activity to see where those rituals might have come from.

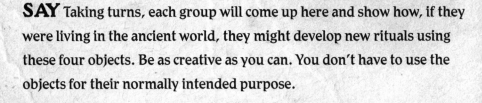 Have students form groups of four.

SAY Taking turns, each group will come up here and show how, if they were living in the ancient world, they might develop new rituals using these four objects. Be as creative as you can. You don't have to use the objects for their normally intended purpose.

→ *Give them a couple of minutes to think about it, and then let them come up in groups. Some of these rituals may be very unusual, so expect laughter.*

ASK · **How meaningful would these rituals be if we actually had to practice them?**

· **Why do you think people historically have invented religious beliefs and practices?**

· **How is faith in Jesus different?**

· **How does it feel to know that you can have a real relationship with the one, true God?**

· **What are some rituals that we practice in the Christian faith that have more meaning than these?**

The Gel...

ASK · **What rituals can we practice this week to keep our hearts and minds focused on Jesus?**

→ *Have the students write down on an index card one thing that tends to come in between them and God. Ask them to think of it as an idol or a false god, something that might distract from their worship. Examples*

MEDIA INFUSION (optional)

Show a clip from *The Empire Strikes Back*. Set the DVD to 1:09:00, when Luke Skywalker says, "We'll never get it out now," and prepare to stop it at 1:12:50, after Yoda lifts the X-Wing out of the swamp.

SAY In this scene, Yoda shows that faith is not governed by size or strength but by a willingness to believe. Roll the clip.

ASK • **What did Luke Skywalker learn from this interaction?**

• **How was the faith of Elijah like Yoda's belief?**

• **How does Jesus show us a similar kind of faith? How can our faith be like this?**

• **What does it feel like to believe and still fail?**

• **What happens when we have faith and succeed?**

might include schoolwork, doubt, a girlfriend or boyfriend, or money. Assure them that what they write is between them and God, and no one else will look at it.

Have students place the notes in a coffee can. Place the can on a flame-resistant surface, like a concrete sidewalk, use a match to light the cards, and let them burn. For larger groups, use only a small handful of cards at a time. If you do not want to burn them, have students place the cards on the ground in front of a lit candle as a symbol of the fact that they are sacrificing them to God.

SAY Just as God was strong enough to light the altar that Elijah built, so God is strong enough to overcome our idols.

→ Have students form pairs, and ask them to pray for one another to have the strength to always put God first.

CLEANING UP

Here are some additional open-ended, thought-provoking questions. Use all or some of them to complement—or even replace—the debriefing questions for any of the activities in this study. You can guide students through this section all together or form smaller discussion groups for more intimate dialogue.

"Well, you know the answer to the question, don't you? Obviously a lot of people are using it to gain votes. Come on. You know that, and I know that. I also don't like constant dedications to children. Give me a break."
—Simon Cowell
(on why *American Idol* contestants talk about God)

· **Why do you think Elijah was so confident?**

· **What's your reaction to the things he said to the priests of Baal?**

· **Why do you think God decided to prove himself in this way?**

· **Why is it sometimes hard to trust God this much?**

· **What happens when we do trust God?**

· **Do you expect God to work miracles when you trust him? Why or why not?**

· **Thinking both of other faiths and of things that people value, what other gods do people worship?**

· **How do you normally respond to people's worship of other gods?**

· **What have you been taught in school and by your family about other people's religious beliefs?**

· **In what situations should we confront those of other beliefs? What are some good ways to do so?**

· **How would you explain to a friend why Jesus can be trusted? How would you describe what it means to be in a close and trustworthy relationship with Jesus?**

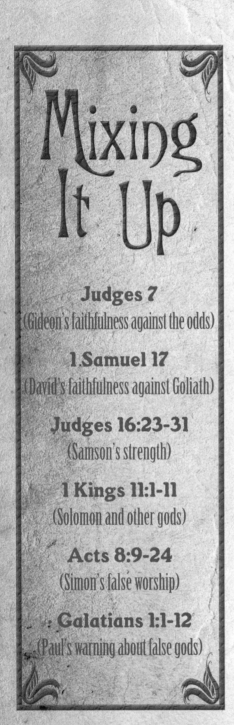

Mixing It Up

Judges 7
(Gideon's faithfulness against the odds)

1 Samuel 17
(David's faithfulness against Goliath)

Judges 16:23-31
(Samson's strength)

1 Kings 11:1-11
(Solomon and other gods)

Acts 8:9-24
(Simon's false worship)

Galatians 1:1-12
(Paul's warning about false gods)

ABOUT GOD

ABOUT PUNISHMENT

ABOUT REQUIREMENTS FOR FOLLOWERS

OTHER DETAILS

Warning: Under God's Orders Prophets Act Strangely

(Ezekiel Follows God's Bizarre——and Gross——Orders)

BIBLE STORY: EZEKIEL 4:1—5:10

❧ ❧

THEME: GOD'S UNEXPECTED PLANS

Subtopics: Scripture, God's Truth, the World, Care for Others, Prophecy

Students will discover how God used Ezekiel to make dramatic statements. They'll also learn more about what prophecy has to do with Jesus, and be challenged to follow God's plan no matter how strange it seems.

SUPPLIES NEEDED:
- one brick or piece of red construction paper for each student
- two dixie (or very small) cups for each student
- pitcher of water
- large glass jar
- Bibles
- mixture of grains (preferably unground) and lentils (include wheat, barley, beans, lentils and millet)
- index cards
- pens
- (optional) Sufjan Stevens' recording *Greetings From Michigan: The Great Lake State*, track 8, "Detroit, Lift Up Your Weary Head," CD player
- hat

PREPARATION AND SETUP:

- Photocopy the handout (p. 60) for each student.
- Move chairs so that you have a large empty space in the center of the room.
- Place the mixture of grains and lentils in the large glass jar.

- Recruit someone to help you distribute supplies and/or direct students during the story time—it could get chaotic if you don't have an assistant!
- (optional) Set Sufjan Steven's CD *Greetings From Michigan: The Great Lake State* to track 8, "Detroit, Lift Up Your Weary Head."

Give one index card and pen or pencil to each student.

SAY We're going to be really creative here. In your mind, think of the strangest command you could give someone. Unfortunately, there have to be some perameters here. The command must be something appropriate, something someone could do in this room without any superpowers or additional supplies. Something like, "Bark like a dog while hopping in a circle on one foot." Once you think of the weirdest command you can, write it on your card, and fold it in half.

➡️ *Give students a few minutes to fill out their cards. When everyone has finished, collect the cards, put them in a hat, mix them up, and pass them out again.*

If you have a small class and you want a little more entertainment, have students take turns doing what's on their cards, rather than simultaneous chaos.

SAY Now, read your card, and on my count of three, everyone do what your card says!

➡️ *Once you've counted to three, give students a few minutes to do what their cards said. When they've finished,*

ASK · How did you feel about doing what was on the card?

· What if God told you directly to do something this weird? What would you think?

SAY Today we're going to learn about God's unexpected plans by reading about someone who did some strange things.

Bizarre Bonus

You can make Ezekiel 4:9 bread! Before or after the study, invite interested students to a house or church kitchen to bake together. Search the Internet for "Ezekiel 4:9 bread" to find a recipe. Purchase ingredients at a health food store if you can't find them at the grocery store. You may also use this bread during the study as a snack for the students to munch on during the story (instead of the lentil/barley mix).

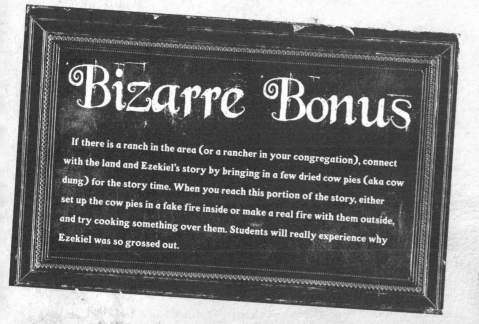

Bizarre Bonus

If there is a ranch in the area (or a rancher in your congregation), connect with the land and Ezekiel's story by bringing in a few dried cow pies (aka cow dung) for the story time. When you reach this portion of the story, either set up the cow pies in a fake fire inside or make a real fire with them outside, and try cooking something over them. Students will really experience why Ezekiel was so grossed out.

pit•tip

Before you start telling the story, set the stage for this strange adventure. Hearing stories from the prophetic books of the Hebrew Scriptures can be an adventure in itself—especially since these are some of the lesser-read books of the Bible. Remind students **who** Ezekiel was (a Jewish prophet and priest preaching to the Hebrew captives in Babylon), **when** this story happened (about 600 B.C.) and the **nature** of biblical prophecy. (The prophet acts as the spokesperson for God's truth. Most of the prophecy in the Old Testament has already been fulfilled because it's about Israel's consequences for disobedience.)

pit•tip

Before you ask students to lie on their left sides, make sure this will not put any girls in skirts in uncomfortable or immodest situations. If you notice that some girls are in skirts, make this an optional activity.

The Guts...

Distribute the bricks (or pieces of red construction paper), map handouts, and pens to all the students.

SAY As I tell the story today, we're going to participate with Ezekiel in a prophetic drama. In this story, God tells Ezekiel what to prophecy while doing specific symbolic actions that demonstrate the future fall of Jerusalem. Though some of the allusions may be unfamiliar to you, remember that they would not be to someone watching and listening to Ezekiel. While you listen to the story, imagine you are Ezekiel. We're going to do modified versions of some of his actions with him—but remember that what he did was much larger and dramatic—and not at all subtle!

First, God told Ezekiel to draw a picture on a brick. So, get your brick (or paper), a map, and a pen. Then draw what Ezekiel had to draw.

And God said to Ezekiel, "And now, son of man, take a large clay brick and set it down in front of you. Then draw a map of the city of Jerusalem on it. Show a city under siege. Build a wall around it so no one can escape. Set up the enemy camp, and surround the city with siege ramps and battering rams."

➜ *Give several minutes for students to draw the picture of the city on their bricks. You may want to read the above paragraph two or three times. You may also want to explain that Ezekiel was making a model—it wasn't just one brick, but a miniature city under siege!*

> "It is unlikely that Ezekiel lay on his side continuously for 390 days. He probably adopted this posture for several hours…at the busiest part of the day. During the rest of the day, especially in the evenings, he probably carried on with his normal activities in the privacy of his home…
> —Daniel I. Block, Wheaton College

Then God said, "Take an iron griddle and place it between you and the city. Turn toward the city and demonstrate how harsh the siege will be against Jerusalem. This will be a warning to the people of Israel."

Then God said, "Now lie on your left side and place the sins of Israel on yourself. You are to bear their sins for the number of days you lie there on your side. I am requiring you to bear Israel's sins for 390 days—one day for each year of their sin. After that, turn over and lie on your right side for 40 days—one day for each year of Judah's sin.

"Meanwhile, keep staring at the siege of Jerusalem. Lie there with your arm bare and prophesy her destruction. I will tie you up with ropes so you won't be able to turn from side to side until the days of your siege have been completed."

➔ *Distribute a small handful of the lentil mix in a small cup to each person. Then continue the story.*

Then God said, "Now go and get some wheat, barley, beans, lentils, millet, and emmer wheat, and mix them together in a storage jar. Use them to make bread for yourself during the 390 days you will be lying on your side. Ration this out to yourself, eight ounces of food for each day, and eat it at set times."

➔ *Give a small cup of water to each student. Once everyone has received a cup of water, continue the story.*

And God said, "Next, measure out a jar of water for each day, and drink it at set times. Prepare and eat this food as you would barley cakes. While all the people are watching, bake it over a fire using dried human dung as fuel, and then eat the bread."

ASK · **How would you respond if God asked you to cook your food using human waste as the fuel?**

➔ *Give students a few minutes to consider and answer this question. Then continue the story.*

Then the Lord said, "This is how Israel will eat defiled bread in the Gentile lands to which I will banish them."
Now we will hear how Ezekiel responded to this command.

➔ *Encourage students to take their map handouts and read the text aloud together. Once they have finished reading Ezekiel's response, continue the story. You may want to explain that this action would have demonstrated Jerusalem's uncleanness before God.*

BELIEVE IT OR NOT

It sounds like Ezekiel may hold the world's record for the longest time a person lay on his or her side. Here are some contemporary records that make what Ezekiel did seem a little less weird:

• Mastram Bapu, an Indian *fakir*, camped out on one spot by the road in Chitra, India for 22 years from 1960 to 1982.

• Rob Colley stayed in a 150-gallon barrel at the top of a 43-foot-high pole in Devon, England for 42 days in 1992.

• Amresh Kumar Jha, also in India, stood on one foot (without holding anything for balance) for 71 hours and 40 minutes in September, 1995. During this time, he did not rest his lifted foot on anything— including the standing foot.

"All right," said the Lord. "You may bake your bread with cow dung instead of human dung." Then he told Ezekiel, "Son of man, I will make food very scarce in Jerusalem. It will be weighed out with great care and eaten fearfully. The water will be rationed out drop by drop, and the people will drink it with dismay. Lacking food and water, people will look at one another in terror, and they will waste away under their punishment.

"Son of man, take a sharp sword and use it as a razor to shave your head and beard. Use a scale to weigh the hair into three equal parts."

Then God said, "Place a third of the hair at the center of your map of Jerusalem. After acting out the siege, burn it there. Scatter another third across your map and chop it with a sword. Scatter the last third to the wind, for I will scatter my people with the sword. Keep just a bit of the hair and tie it up in your robe. Then take some of these hairs out and throw them into the fire, burning them up. A fire will then spread from this remnant and destroy all of Israel."

Then God said, "This is what the Sovereign Lord says: This is an illustration of what will happen to Jerusalem. I placed her at the center of the nations, but she has rebelled against my regulations and decrees and has been even more wicked than the surrounding nations. She has refused to obey the regulations and decrees I gave her to follow."

ASK · How did you feel hearing and acting out this story?

· Why do you think that God told Ezekiel to act this out rather than simply telling the people what was going to happen?

· How can seeing or doing something be more meaningful than just hearing words?

· How do you imagine people responded to Ezekiel? How would you respond to Ezekiel?

· Why isn't following God's unexpected plans safe? comfortable? predictable? What do we risk by obeying God?

MEDIA INFUSION
(optional)
Together, listen to Sufjan Steven's song, "Detroit, Lift Up Your Weary Head."
SAY Both this song and the Ezekiel passage are about cities that the speaker (or singer) knows well—and both seem to care about these cities.
ASK • How do you think Jesus wants our attitudes and actions toward our own communities to be?
• What are practical ways we can show our care for our communities?

- Israel had sinned, and wandered from God. Think for a moment about your sin, or any way you're wandering from God. How can you turn back toward God in this area?
- How do you connect God's perfect love with the destruction he was about to bring about in this passage?

➡ *Make sure students keep their supplies from this activity—they will be used again later in the study.*

pit·tip

Toward the end of study, you may consider pointing students toward the fulfillment of the prophecy in Ezekiel 4. It's important that teenagers see that God was faithful in carrying out what he intended. You can find prophecy fulfillment in Lamentations (primarily chapters three and four), where terrible famine and death is described.

The Grit... **SAY This is a pretty weird passage. You could study it for a long time before you felt secure in saying what it meant. We're going to take a few moments to really dig into another passage and figure out what we can take away from it.**

Ezekiel was a prophet most of us probably don't know much about. But we do know more about another prophet: Jesus.

➡ *Instruct students to turn to Matthew 26:31-35. Ask several students to read the passage aloud.*

pit·tip

If you have the time and materials, consider having students act out even more of the story—or the whole thing. Figure out what works best for your group. For instance, rather than shaving their heads (which we wouldn't recommend!), they can cut a small piece of hair or pull several hairs out. Or, alternately, one staff member can act out Ezekiel's drama while you read the story and the students can watch.

SAY In this passage Jesus prophesies Peter's betrayal. Peter has a hard time believing what Jesus says. But Jesus is right: Peter does betray him three times.

pit·tip

You might use some biblical resources to help students better understand Ezekiel's context—and how his story might impact their relationship with God.

Divide students into small groups, or some students may work individually if they prefer. Provide them with the resources. Write the questions on page 59 in a place where everyone can see them. These will be the leading questions for students' exploration. Let them know that they are not required to find answers to all the questions, but that these questions should help guide what they learn.

Thankfully, there are a lot of resources out there to assist Christians in their study of the Bible. To prepare for this section, collect a variety of Bible dictionaries, commentaries on Ezekiel (make sure they're written for lay people and aren't highly academic!), and Bible handbooks. Borrow books from your pastor, the church library, or others in your congregation. *Select resources that will be accessible to **your** students.* If you can only find one or two resources, that is OK. Simply seek publisher permission to photocopy the applicable pages on this passage.

ASK · Name the emotions Peter was probably feeling. When have you felt this way, either when it comes to your relationship with Jesus, or something else?

· What connections can you make between this passage and Ezekiel's story?

· What does this story of Jesus' prophecy and Peter's betrayal reveal about Jesus?

· In what ways is Jesus different from other prophets? Why is this significant to you and your relationship with Jesus?

· What's on the other end of obedience to God's unexpected plans?

The Gel...

Instruct the students to gather their brick, lentil mix, cup, and pen from the story activity earlier in the study. Students will use these supplies to construct, design, or symbolize an aspect of their lives by which they may demonstrate obedience to God. Encourage students to be quiet, and only take a few minutes for students to assemble their prayers. Then, moving around the room, pray with each student individually. Students may say their own prayers (short!) or simply pray, "Jesus, your plans are often unexpected. Despite how scared, stubborn, or confused I might be...I want to love you, obey you, and follow you with my life. Please help me to do this by _____."

CLEANING UP

BEGIN CLEANING UP

Here are some additional open-ended, thought-provoking questions. Use all or some of them to complement—or even replace—the debriefing questions for any of the activities in this study. You can guide students through this section all together, or form smaller discussion groups for more intimate dialogue.

· What do you know about the situation with Israel and Judah?

· What do you think are the symbolic meanings of any or all of the following: the brick (or tile), the griddle, the model of the siege, the food and water, the food preparation, and the hair?

· How are prophecy and fortune-telling different?

· In Scripture, we're warned not to participate in fortune-telling, but there's a lot of prophecy. How can we understand this disconnect?

· Why do you think it's so hard for people to believe some of these prophecies we've heard today?

· What does this story of Ezekiel teach you about the Bible in general?

· What have you discovered about God's plans? Do you think they're always, sometimes, or never unexpected? Why or why not?

· How would you explain to someone else why a relationship with Jesus is the key to God's plan?

· Why is it important to God that we obey him no matter what? How is obedience to God like or unlike obedience to people here on earth?

· How has God called you to uniquely obey him? What will you do?

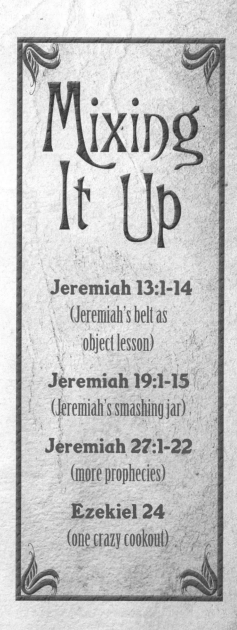

Mixing It Up

Jeremiah 13:1-14
(Jeremiah's belt as object lesson)

Jeremiah 19:1-15
(Jeremiah's smashing jar)

Jeremiah 27:1-22
(more prophecies)

Ezekiel 24
(one crazy cookout)

"O Sovereign Lord, must I be defiled by using human dung? For I have never been defiled before. From the time I was a child until now I have never eaten any animal that died of sickness or was killed by other animals. I have never eaten any meat forbidden by the law."

Ezekiel 4:14

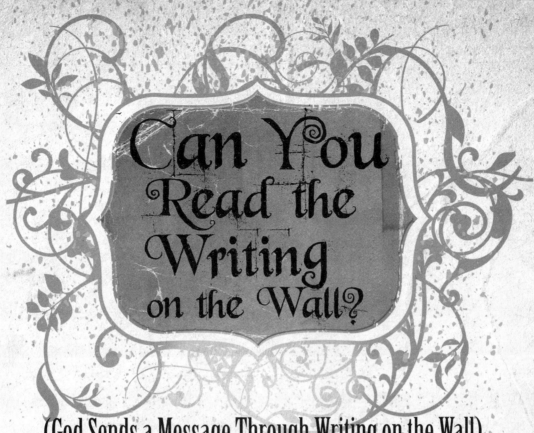

Can You Read the Writing on the Wall?

(God Sends a Message Through Writing on the Wall)

BIBLE STORY: DANIEL 5:1-31

THEME: CHOICES AND CONSEQUENCES

Subtopics: Truth, Wisdom, Secrets, God's Promises

Students will explore the story of King Belshazzar, who learned about choices the tough way. As they dig into the story of the writing on the wall, students will discover that there are consequences for their choices and that it's important to look to God for the right choices.

SUPPLIES NEEDED:
- pens
- 8.5" x 11" sheets of paper for each student
- two pieces of newsprint (roughly 3'x3')

PREPARATION AND SETUP:
- Make sure the room can be cleared of any tables or chairs, so students can sit on the floor.

- two pieces of tape
- two markers
- (optional) TV and DVD player, movie *Signs*
- Bibles

- Each student will need a pen and a piece of paper.
- Make a copy of "The Writing on My Wall" handout (p. 70) for every student.

• (optional) Set up a TV and DVD player, and cue the movie *Signs* to show the scene beginning in Chapter 10 at 0:41:15 when Joaquin Phoenix's character says: "Some people are probably thinking this is the end of the world." You'll end the clip at 0:43:40 when Mel Gibson's character says: "Is it possible that there are no coincidences?"

SAY To understand the weird Bible story we'll explore today, we'll begin with an activity that will require some interpreting.

SAY Form groups of five to seven, and sit in a circle. Each of you should have a piece of paper and a pen. When we begin, each person will sketch a picture of some activity or scene that begins a story. This could be as simple as a person skiing down a hill or three children sitting in chairs. Draw small, since this paper will be added to several times.

At 30 seconds, I will say "pass" and you will pass your paper to your left and immediately (without talking) the person with the paper will write a caption underneath the picture you see. Don't ask your neighbor what it is he or she meant to draw—you must interpret the picture yourself. For example, if you are passed a picture of a person skiing down a hill, you may write underneath, "Jim loves skiing right after a fresh snowfall," or, "Mary can't feel her fingers anymore, it's so cold on the mountain."

After another 30 seconds, pass the paper again to your left, quickly read the caption, and draw a second picture that continues that story. You will continue passing until each person receives the original paper they began with.

 After everyone has had a chance to contribute to the story, discuss.

SAY Take a look at your original picture. Read the captions and look at the pictures that were added to create a story.

- • How did this activity show the importance of choice?
- • What were the consequences of each new direction for the story?
- • How is this activity like or unlike following God's will by making the

pit·tip

If you have a small class, and you want a little more entertainment, have students take turns doing what's on their cards rather than simultaneous chaos.

right choices in our lives?

• How easy or difficult is it for you to figure out what choices God wants you to make? What do you think happens when we don't make the right choices?

• How did this activity show the importance of choice?

SAY As we read the story of the writing on the wall, think about how important our every choice is—not just because of the possible consequences, but because focusing on trusting God with every choice makes the best sense for our lives.

Ask for two volunteers to keep a tally of the "good decisions" and "bad decisions" King Belshazzar makes throughout the story. Write the words "good decisions" on one piece of newsprint and tape it on the right side of the front wall. Write the words "bad decisions" on the second piece of newsprint and tape it on the left side of the front wall. Volunteers will mark the appropriate paper for good and bad decisions made by King Belshazzar. As you read through the story, make sure to pause when instructed for effect.

SAY Today's study centers around the famous Old Testament story of the writing on the wall. As I read, pay attention to the good and bad decisions King Belshazzar makes. When I pause, we will decide whether he has made a good or bad decision, and our two volunteers will keep a tally.

Sometime after King Nebuchadnezzar's reign, a King named Belshazzar ruled Babylon and all of Jerusalem. During a night of drunken feasting with his nobles, wives, concubines, and servants, Belshazzar got the great idea to use gold and silver cups taken from the Temple in Jerusalem to toast his reign. *(Pause)*

His servants brought him the cups, and the whole party began drinking, toasting idols and gods made of gold, silver, and bronze. *(Pause)*

At that moment, a human hand began writing on the palace wall. Just four words. Mene. Mene. Tekel. Parsin. Belshazzar was absolutely terrified—so much so that he literally fell over. *(Pause)*

He asked his astrologers and fortunetellers to interpret the meaning of the writing. But no one could decipher it. *(Pause)*

It was at this time that his mother remembered Daniel and advised her son to call him. Belshazzar called for Daniel and promised him wealth and power if he could interpret the words on the palace wall. *(Pause)*

Daniel refused the wealth and the power but delivered God's message to Belshazzar. Daniel condemned the King for not heeding the wisdom of his predecessor, King Nebuchadnezzar, saying that he had not humbled himself before the Lord. *(Pause)*

Daniel then said that Belshazzar had violated the gold and silver cups from the Temple by using them to worship other gods. *(Pause)*

Then Daniel interpreted the words, which meant:

Mene, Mene: your days are numbered

Tekel: you have failed the test

Parsin: your kingdom has been divided

When he heard the prophecy, Belshazzar proclaimed Daniel the third-highest ruler in the kingdom. *(Pause)*

That very night, Belshazzar was slain by his enemies, who had broken into the palace. *(Pause)*

ASK · **What was King Belshazzar's biggest mistake?**

· **What else can we assume about Belshazzar's reign based on his behavior?**

· **Why do you think God chose to deliver his message to Belshazzar in this way?**

· **Does God's punishment seem harsh, fair, understandable, scary, or something else to you? Explain.**

· **What can we learn from this story about trusting God in making choices? What about his promises?**

SAY God is an absolutely fair, perfect Father. He loves us and wants us to make the best choices. And, because he is perfect, God always keeps his promises. After reading this story of Belshazzar's downfall, the possible consequences for bad choices might seem intimidating…even scary. But, God is full of grace, and he loves you—so much that he sent his Son Jesus to die for your sins. We have nothing to be afraid of when we are in an intimate, growing relationship with Jesus. We can rely on him and know that he'll do what he says he will do. And he will help you trust him in following his will. Let's explore this concept some more.

look to God for right choices – wrong choices won't have such harsh consequences

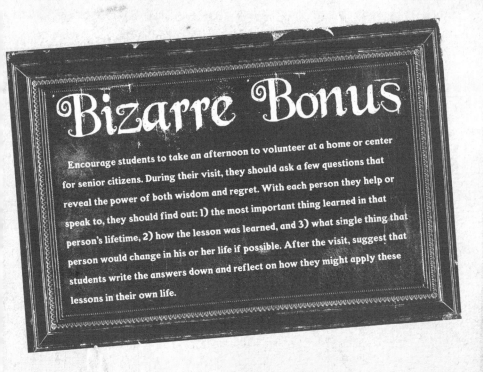

Bizarre Bonus

Encourage students to take an afternoon to volunteer at a home or center for senior citizens. During their visit, they should ask a few questions that reveal the power of both wisdom and regret. With each person they help or speak to, they should find out: 1) the most important thing learned in that person's lifetime, 2) how the lesson was learned, and 3) what single thing that person would change in his or her life if possible. After the visit, suggest that students write the answers down and reflect on how they might apply these lessons in their own life.

The Grit… Designate each corner of the room as either: Strongly Agree, Agree, Disagree, or Strongly Disagree. You may do this by just pointing or taping a piece of paper in each corner. You will read the following statements one at a time and ask students to choose the corner that corresponds to their belief. For example, if they strongly agree with the statement they go to the strongly agree corner, and so on. Those who are undecided will go to the middle of the room.

BELIEVE IT OR NOT

It seems everyone is looking for signs these days—signs that offer insight into their lives, signs that show them the right way to turn, or signs that just give them hope. Consider what transpired during 2003 at a hospital outside Boston, where hundreds of people gathered each evening to see what could only be described as a vision of the Virgin Mary. A dirty window revealed this apparent apparition to crowds of sign-seekers and believers. Onlookers had differing views of the vision, some saying it was a sign from God, others that it just needed to be cleaned, and still others that it gave them hope. Perhaps the real oddity of this phenomenon was that the people kept coming. The hospital had to cover the window during business hours so the crowds wouldn't interfere with hospital business. One gatherer wisely commented that the true miracle of this sign would be the act of a person seeing the window who was then inspired to approach their worst enemy and ask for forgiveness.

MEDIA INFUSION
(optional)

Watch a clip from *Signs*. You'll start in Chapter 10 at 0:41:15 when Joaquin Phoenix's character says: "Some people are probably thinking this is the end of the world." End at 0:43:40 when Mel Gibson's character says: "Is it possible that there are no coincidences?"

In this scene, two brothers discuss their views on miracles and, more specifically, whether life is a series of coincidences or the result of a divine plan.

SAY This clip from *Signs* explores the complex human reaction to the bizarre, the confusing, and the unexplained.

ASK • Based on the description of the two categories of people in this clip, where do you think King Belshazzar belongs? Daniel? Why?

• What category do you fall into? Why?

Once students have selected a corner, they will prepare their reasoning with others in their corner and will try to convince the rest of the group to join their group. Encourage students to have some fun with this and not be too aggressive in their reasoning.

You'll allow two or three minutes for groups to prepare their statements and up to five minutes for each group to convince other corners. When all groups have spoken, students have the opportunity to switch their positions. This activity will encourage deep discussion, so don't be afraid to let groups disagree, but keep a tight lead on the focus of the conversation.

• **SAY** The story of the writing on the wall reveals the consequences of ignoring God's plan and will for our lives. I will read you a statement that relates to this story, and you need to decide whether you strongly agree, agree, disagree, or strongly disagree. Choose your corner and prepare your reasoning. Those who are undecided may sit in the middle.

• **SAY** Like the writing on the wall, God does miracles today to get people's attention.

➜ *Allow students to choose a corner (or the middle), and prepare and present their reasoning.*

_____

• **SAY** I learn the most in my relationship with God through his discipline.

➜ *Allow students to choose a corner (or the middle), and prepare and present their reasoning.*

_____

• **SAY** All choices are equally important to me.

➡ *Allow students to choose a corner (or the middle), and prepare and present their reasoning.*

pit•tip

Encourage students to apply this prayer specifically to their life. Before they pray, they may want to ask themselves: "What am I currently struggling with that needs God's wisdom?"

SAY Daniel had a long history of delivering messages of God's promise. Before Belshazzar was king, Babylon was ruled by Nebuchadnezzar, who was confounded by some troubling dreams. Daniel was called upon to interpret the meaning of these dreams—and if he was unsuccessful, King Nebuchadnezzar would kill him. When Daniel sought God's help, God explained the meaning of these dreams, and Daniel praised God for his faithfulness.

➡ *Ask students to think of a situation in their life that requires guidance and insight into God's promises. Individually, students will pray through the prayer of Nebuchadnezzar (Daniel 2:20-23), while asking for God to make his will for them clear.*

"Praise the name of God forever and ever, for he has all wisdom and power. He determines the course of world events; he removes kings and sets up other kings. He gives wisdom to the wise and knowledge to the scholars. He reveals deep and mysterious things and knows what lies hidden in darkness, though he is surrounded by light. I thank and praise you, God of my ancestors, for you have given me wisdom and strength…"

The Gel...

Suggest to your students that the story of King Belshazzar offers a unique insight into how we might better follow Jesus. Remind them that King Belshazzar ignored the wisdom of his predecessor, King Nebuchadnezzar, and because of this left himself open to God's discipline. While we shouldn't live in fear, honest assessment of our walk with God is an important part of our faith.

For this activity, distribute "The Writing on My Wall" handout

(p. 70) to each student. Allow 10 minutes for students to begin filling out this page. Encourage students to go back and use the handout in the future. They can put it in a place they will remember, like in their Bible or in a school notebook.

CLEANING UP

Here are some additional open-ended, thought-provoking questions. Use all or some of them to complement—or even replace—the debriefing questions for any of the activities in this study. You can guide students through this section all together, or form smaller discussion groups for more intimate dialogue.

- What do the four words written on the wall reveal about King Belshazzar's reign?
- Based on the story, what reasons are given for why God dethroned King Belshazzar?
- What should King Belshazzar have learned from his predecessor, King Nebuchadnezzar?
- Why do you think the taking of the "gold and silver cups" (v. 2) is such a sin?
- What might be a modern equivalent to this sin? Why does this anger God?

"The consequences of our actions grab us by the scruff of our necks, quite indifferent to our claim that we have 'gotten better' in the meantime."
—Friedrich Nietzsche

· Why doesn't King Belshazzar know who Daniel is?

· This story reveals the consequences of responding to God's will too late. In what ways have you been ignoring God's wisdom in your life?

· What does this story reveal about how God follows through on his promises? Why is this significant to you in your faith?

· What character are you most like in this story? (Daniel, King Belshazzar, the king's mother, a soldier) Why?

· Daniel's faith in God's wisdom is evident throughout this story. When you encounter tough times, do you ask for God's wisdom in making choices? Why or why not?

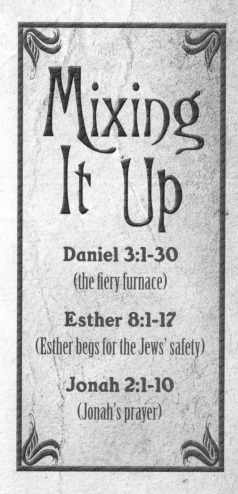

Mixing It Up

Daniel 3:1-30
(the fiery furnace)

Esther 8:1-17
(Esther begs for the Jews' safety)

Jonah 2:1-10
(Jonah's prayer)

THE WRITING ON MY WALL

King Belshazzar ignored God's will for his life by ignoring the wisdom of his predecessor, King Nebuchadnezzar. Because of this, he faced serious consequences, which included: losing his kingdom, his throne, and his life—all in one night. While we shouldn't react with fear to this example, it's a good reminder of how we can trust God when we make choices. He loves us completely and knows what's best for us, so we can trust that he'll guide us to the right choices.

Be quiet and reflect for a few moments…What might God be wanting to tell you about your own life? In what ways are you listening or not listening?

Take a quiet moment to complete this sheet. Keep it in your Bible to remind you that God knows everything about your life and wants to guide you through the tough times.

Big Issues: *What are the most challenging situations you currently face?*

-
-
-

God's Wisdom: *How have you asked God to guide you through this?*

-
-
-

Writing on Your Wall: *What has God revealed to you about these things?*

-
-
-

The Road Ahead: *What choices will you make to trust and follow God?*

-
-
-

A Fishy Story

(Big Fish Swallows Jonah)

BIBLE STORY: JONAH 1:1-17

THEME: GOD'S RELENTLESS LOVE

Subtopics: Trust, Obedience, Decision-Making, God's Will

Students will study the story of Jonah in the fish's belly, and learn how much God loves them and wants the best for them…even if his actions seem a little strange.

SUPPLIES NEEDED:

- a kiddie pool (try asking congregation members for a loaner) or large container (it should be able to be lifted)
- liquid starch
- white glue
- green food coloring
- roll of plastic wrap
- a slipper
- a bottle of hair gel
- one index card and one pen for each student
- a container to hold all of the index cards
- (optional) computer with an Internet connection
- (optional) video projection unit
- Bibles
- oversized clothes

PREPARATION AND SETUP:

- Make three copies of the handout (p. 80).
- Mix into the kiddie pool (or largest container you can find) one part liquid starch, one part water, and one part white glue. As an added bonus, use a little green food coloring. The pool should be about three-quarters full. If you can, warn the students ahead of time to wear clothes that they can get dirty. Bring some extra, oversized clothes in case they forget.
- If you're not using a kiddie pool for "The Goo…" and "The Guts…" activities, consider videotaping yourself doing the storytelling while sitting in the pool. You'll play this video for the group instead of doing everything live.
- Cover a slipper in hair gel (this is your "fish"), and cut enough 10 foot pieces of plastic wrap for each pair of students to have one.
- Make four photocopies of the sketch handout (p. 80) —one for you, and one for each student actor
- (optional) set up a computer with Internet connect and a TV or projector on which to show the online video.

The Goo…

Stand near the kiddie pool (or large container).

SAY As you may know, the coolest part of the story of Jonah is not that he was called to an impossible mission and not that an entire city changed direction because of him, it was that he got to bathe in fish snot. Today, you get to do the same. Fortunately, I keep a pet whale in my swimming pool at home, and I was able to get him to blow his nose just before I came today.

→ *If you have a kiddie pool filled with the ingredients and you've warned the teenagers to dress for this activity, have them form two teams and run a relay race of sorts—where each person ends by diving into the mixture.*

If you have a smaller container, do this alternative activity: ask students to stand in a straight line and pass the container (with the same mixture inside) down the line from the front to the back; the goal is to get as much of the contents to the last person as possible. Of course, there will be some spilling.

Afterward, have an adult leader or volunteer take the kiddie pool, rinse it, and fill it halfway with water. This should be done during the following conversation, since you'll need this pool for the next activity. However, if you don't have a kiddie pool on hand (if you used a container for this opening experience), disregard.

pit·tip

Youth games are a thin line between fun and function. It's important that the students have a blast getting involved in the games because, for some of them, that involvement is what really draws them to church. It also gives them something to talk about when they invite their friends to church. On the other hand, the games should draw students into some aspect of the study in a concrete way. For games like this, let them get immersed in the fun, but make sure you have their full attention as you begin to discuss Jonah's powerful story.

ASK · What would you do to avoid handling real fish snot?

· Think about a time when you've been cold, uncomfortable, or even in pain. When is it worth it to put up with a really uncomfortable situation?

· If God told you to go somewhere that you didn't want to go, how much would you do to get out of it? Or would you just go? Why?

· How might a relationship with Jesus change the things that God calls us to, even when we don't want to do them?

· Why might God asking us to do something strange show that his love is relentless? What does that word mean to you?

Bizarre Bonus

Encourage your students to spend some time in a reasonably small space thinking about God, just as Jonah did. Tell them to find a quiet enclosed space, like a closet (preferably without a lock) or a small laundry room. Tell them to try to sit there alone until they really wish they were somewhere else. Then encourage them to spend some more time thinking about what it means to be alone with Jesus.

BELIEVE IT OR NOT
Fin whales can use their tail flukes to destroy whaling boats. Whale: one point, whale killers: no points. Killer whales, on the other hand, aren't really human killers and aren't responsible for the most common kinds of whale attacks on humans, though they have been known to eat things as big as a blue whale!

The Guts...

Distribute the handout (p. 80) to three students. They can be volunteers or people you think will do a good job with the sketch.

→ *There are a couple of ideal ways to tell this story. If you're using a kiddie pool, go ahead and have the actors sit in the water. If you're not using a pool, play the video you created. Either way, the following is what your students will experience.*

SAY You've heard the story of Jonah and the whale, but you may not realize what was going on in Jonah's mind. Jonah was told to go to Nineveh, the capital of Assyria. Assyria was an enemy of Israel, Jonah's people. Later on in the story, Assyria would actually take over most of the land that the Israelites owned. Being told to go to Nineveh would be like being told to go sit at the lunch table full of snobbish bullies who always make fun of you when you walk past, and try to make friends with them.

You can see why he ran.

Sure enough, off in the other direction he went. This is the part of the story most of us have heard. Instead of getting away with it, God was on Coast Guard duty and caught him like a bad pirate in foreign waters. Fortunately, the kind and gracious men on the boat realized it would be in Jonah's best interests to go for a long swim.

Here's the miracle. A big fish gobbled Jonah up, deep in its belly, past the grinding teeth, down the tight squeeze of the throat, into the pit of stomach acid. Yet somehow Jonah was spit out three days later with nothing but a grudge and an odd, new body odor.

You may wonder what happened in those three days. Well, as a matter of fact, I happened to be there, and I happened to have my trusty video camera, and this is what I caught on tape.

→ *Introduce the three actors playing Jonah, Fish 1, and Fish 2. Then have them read together the sketch on the handout (p. 80).*

Jonah went to preach to the Ninevites anyway, because A) he didn't want another free ride in the oily submarine, and B) he left his bus pass on the boat. When Jonah preached to the Ninevites, they actually changed. They repented and turned away from their failures. Now here's the part of the story your Sunday school teacher might not have told you: Jonah, rather than putting on a party hat and shooting off fireworks, went to the corner to sulk. Jonah was really hoping that, after all the work he had done, God would send a lightning bolt as kind of an exclamation point at the end of his sermon. He really wanted God to judge the Ninevites. They were, after all, bullies who had gotten away with the lives that they led for far too long. Instead, God forgave them. It looked like God had really made Jonah's preaching effective.

Jonah didn't trust God to send him in the right direction, and he didn't trust God to make the right decisions once he got there. So, ironically, even though Jonah was successful by all appearances, he was sad at the end of the day.

Sometimes a relationship with Jesus is not something we had planned for our own lives, but that is exactly what God calls us to. Sometimes Jesus will then call us further into mission and ministry, into relationships with difficult people, into serving the poor. All of this may seem challenging, but Jesus calls us into the life of faith out of love for us. And his love is relentless. But that doesn't mean it's always comfortable, as Jonah could tell us.

→ *Have students form groups of four, and ask them to share with one another something in their lives or in their futures about which they're anxious or having trouble trusting God.*

ASK · What makes it hard for you to trust that God loves you relentlessly?

· When might we be unhappy or uncomfortable with God's decisions? How might that reveal his love for us even more?

· What might help you to be more at peace with God's leading? better understand how much he loves you?

· How might obeying God—no matter what he's called you to do—draw you closer to him?

SAY Sometimes things happen that make no good sense, and it's hard to see God's plan in them, and it's even harder to know how to respond. But God is in control, and he loves all of his people with a creative, relentless love. We might not always understand or even agree with God's decisions, but we are valuable to him, and we cannot escape from his love.

pit · tip

When giving a talk to students, you have to do a fair amount of observation of their responses as you deliver your message. You want to keep an eye out for distracted students, students whose eyes are droopy, and people who look like they don't want to be there. It is a challenge to keep them involved, but you can do so in a few ways: by addressing them directly in the middle of your talk ("Sarah and I once had a conversation about something like this") or by standing near them. You have to be alert to when your message is losing most of your audience, and that might be a time to switch to an activity and return to the message later.

 **For this activity, you'll need the fake "fish" you created earlier, made with a slipper and hair gel. You'll also need a roll of plastic wrap.**

SAY Everyone is going to need to stand in a circle. Since we've already handled whale goo today, I wouldn't think of making you touch a fish. However, your friends might be thinking about it. We're going to play a little game. We'll need two or three people to lie down in the middle of the circle at a time. Your friends will then use strips of plastic wrap to toss the "fish" around over your heads.

ASK · Looking around this circle right now, how do you feel about trusting them to juggle a fish over your head?

➡️ *Ask for two or three volunteers to lay down on their backs in the middle of the circle. Then have people in the circle stretch out long strips of plastic wrap between them and over the top of the people lying down, one person on each end of a sheet that is around five to ten feet long. The strips should go across the center of the circle like spokes on a wheel.*

SAY I'm going to place the "fish" on one of the strips of plastic wrap. The goal of the people in the circle is to pass the fish from one strip to another until it has balanced for a second or two on each strip. If it falls, the person on the floor to whom it lands the closest (or on whom it lands) can rotate into the circle, and the person who dropped it can lay down on the floor.

→ *Allow this to go on for a while. The game is fairly easy, with the exception of the fact that laughter tends to make the fish fall a lot.*

ASK · For those of you on the floor, as you see a huge, wet slimy thing flying towards you, how does that make you feel?

· Was it hard to trust your friends standing around you? Why or why not?

· When you have to do something difficult, challenging, or scary, how do you react? Is that like or unlike how you *should* react? Explain.

· Have you ever had experiences that made it hard to believe that God loves you and wants the best for you?

· What events in your life right now make it hard to experience God's relentless love?

· How do we accept God's love and follow him despite these things?

The Gel...

Distribute markers, and ask students to draw a fish on the backs of their hands to help them remember to meditate on their need to believe in and experience God's relentless love during the week.

For the following activity, you will need a container that you can keep hidden away in a corner of the church for a year, index cards, and pens.

MEDIA INFUSION (optional)

Find the news video clip taken in Oregon of a whale that washed up on the beach in Florence, Oregon in 1970. It is readily available on Youtube.com and at various places on the Web. The whale had died and could not be moved, removed, or buried—so the Oregon Highway Division decided to blow it up with a half-ton of dynamite. The video has circled the globe ever since then. It's a little scary, a bit gross, super-weird, and very funny (especially the news commentator's coverage of the event). Preview the video before showing it to your group.

Afterward, talk about how God's working in our life can be scary, weird, even funny—but it has a purpose, and always reflects his love for us.

SAY Just as Jonah was in the belly of the fish for a while, let's put some of our prayers in safe-keeping for a year and see what happens. Write down a prayer request on an index card, especially if there's an area where you need to believe that God relentlessly loves you. We'll lock these prayer requests up and open them in a year to see what God has done in our lives.

➡ *Place the container somewhere accessible but out of the way, like a storage room or attic. Mark the date on top, and write yourself a note to remember this next year.*

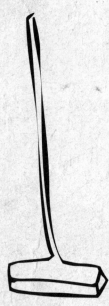

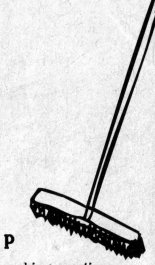

CLEANING UP

Here are some additional open-ended, thought-provoking questions. Use all or some of them to complement—or even replace—the debriefing questions for any of the activities in this study. You can guide students through this section all together, or form smaller discussion groups for more intimate dialogue.

· **Do you feel sympathy for Jonah? Why or why not?**

· **Do you think you would have obeyed God's call to Nineveh or run away? Explain.**

· **Can you think of anything to which God has called you that you don't really want to do? How did this reflect God's love for you?**

· **How far can we resist God's will?**

· **Why might God want us to share our faith with people we**

"Do fish ever get seasick?"
—James Joyce, *Ulysses*

BEGIN CLEANING UP

don't like? How can we show God's relentless love to others in this way?

· Do you think it would have been better if God had punished the Ninevites instead of sending Jonah to preach to them? Why or why not?

· What makes it hard to trust that God loves us completely?

· What might be the best and worst things to happen if we were always open to God's relentless love?

· What might Jesus be calling you to in your life right now? How will it affect your relationship with him?

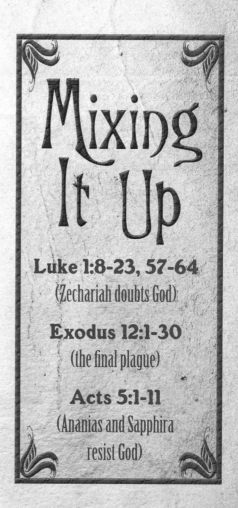

Mixing It Up

Luke 1:8-23, 57-64
(Zechariah doubts God)

Exodus 12:1-30
(the final plague)

Acts 5:1-11
(Ananias and Sapphira resist God)

JONAH AND THE FISHES: A SKETCH

JONAH: *(gasping for air)* Where am l?

FISH 1: You're here!

JONAH: Where's the boat?

FISH 2: It's there.

JONAH: Where there?

FISH 1: Not here.

JONAH: Why would God dump me in a dark cave?

FISH 1: He thinks he's in a cave.

FISH 2: He thinks it's God's fault.

JONAH: Isn't it? He was the one who sent me here.

FISH 1: l believe he sent you in just about exactly the opposite direction.

JONAH: Well, yeah, but…

FISH 2: There's always a but.

JONAH: He told me to go where l didn't want to.

FISH 1: *(sarcastically)* Oh right, shame on God.

FISH 2: *(sarcastically)* Oh right, shame on God.

JONAH: It sounds silly when you say it that way.

FISH 1: Your version wasn't exactly brilliant.

JONAH: So if this isn't a cave, what is it?

FISH 2: It's where you end up when you go the opposite way from God's way.

JONAH: Wait…l'm in hell?

FISH 2: It is for a fish, l'll tell you that.

Jesus Heals: Thousands Flee in Panic

(Jesus Orders Evil Spirits Out of Man—Into Pigs)

BIBLE STORY: MARK 5:1-20; LUKE 8:26-39

Luke 8:27-33
34-39

THEME: JESUS' POWER
Subtopics: Pain, Demons, Fear, Control, Submission

Students will learn about the power Jesus has over all creation—including demons. After the study, students will be empowered to commit more of their lives and experiences into Jesus' hands.

SUPPLIES NEEDED:
- two flashlights
- several Bible concordances (one for every five to seven students. They don't have to all be the same version; use what you can find or what your church prefers.)
- Bibles
- one fabric or rag scrap for each student
- one adhesive bandage for each student
- one rock for each student
- two paper clips in a chain for each student
- (optional) logs, theatrical gels, s'mores fixings, or a candle
- (optional) CD player, Danielson's *Ships* album, track 2, "Cast It at the Setting Sail"

PREPARATION AND SETUP:

- If your room has windows and it's light outside, close the window shades. If you don't have window shades, tape paper to the windows to darken the room.
- Photocopy the handouts (pp. 90-91) for every student.

- Find four different containers (bowls, shoe boxes, etc.) for the scraps, bandages, rocks, and paper clips and place the items in the bowls. (Keep them separate from one another; don't mix them up!)
- (optional) Cue Danielson's *Ships* album to track 2, "Cast It at the Setting Sail."

The Goo...

Before the students arrive, turn off all the lights. As they enter, invite them to sit in a circle and tell stories.

SAY I'm sure you've all been to a campfire where people take turns telling scary stories. We're going to have a little storytelling now, but I'm looking for true stories that happened to you or your family or friends... true scary stories.

→ *Explain to the students that you're going to have a fast-forward campfire experience. One flashlight will be passed around the circle. When you receive the flashlight, you may either tell a short, true, scary story or pass the flashlight to your neighbor. No matter where you are in your story, you must pass the flashlight to your neighbor when the leader's flashlight goes off! (In the event that no one has something to share, make sure that you or another staff member can pull one out of your sleeve.)*

Once the flashlight has been passed around the circle,

SAY True scary stories are nothing new. Today we're going to learn about a strange event that happened to Jesus.

pit·tip

Make a real—or almost real—campfire with logs, orange, yellow, or red theatrical gels (those clear plastic things that go over lights). You could even serve s'mores (real or the microwave kind). Or, if this study will be presented at night, do this part outside where you can sit around a real campfire.

If this is too much work, you can always set a candle in the center for ambience. Just make sure whatever you do isn't breaking a fire code!

The Guts...

Distribute the photocopies of the dialogue handout (p. 91).

SAY We're going to tell today's story together. I will tell the story, but you all have lines or sounds to make. You'll take turns reading the lines by passing the flashlight around as we did before. When I lift up my flashlight, you'll know it's time for the next line.

→ *As you tell the story, gesture at each character so that they can participate when it's time.*

SAY After a rather scary boat ride, Jesus and the disciples arrived on shore. As soon as Jesus climbed out of the boat, a demon-possessed man came running out from the cemetery to meet him. He was crazy. He was dirty. He was naked. Though officially homeless, he had made the burial caves his home. Everyone was afraid of him—they had tried to chain him up but the crazy man would just snap the chains from his wrists and smash the shackles. He spent his time wandering around among the caves, howling and cutting his skin up with sharp stones.

As soon as Jesus saw the man (even though he was far away) he said… *(cue #1: "Come out of this man, you evil spirit!")*.

When the man reached Jesus he bowed low before him. Then he said… *(cue #2: "Why are you interfering with me, Jesus, Son of the Most High God? In the name of God, I beg you, don't torture me!")*.

Then Jesus asked the man… *(cue #3: "What is your name?")*.

The man said… *(cue #4: "My name is Legion because there are many of us inside this man.")* Then, the demons started begging Jesus.

(cue #5: ad lib "Please, please don't send us away! I want to stay right here. I hate to travel, etc.") So Jesus agreed not to send them far away. *(cue #6: "OK. Be gone from this man. Go into the pigs if you wish.")*

The evil spirits went out of the man and into a herd of 2,000 pigs that was rooting about nearby. The pigs ran down a hill *(cue #7: raucous pig sounds)*, **into the lake and drowned** *(cue #8: drowning pig sounds)*.

The pig herders ran to a nearby town, spreading the news about what happened… *(cue #9: ad lib, "We lost our pigs! Demons went into them and then the pigs drowned! What are we going to do for work now?"*

pit·tip

If you are afraid of the prospect of a scary-story free-for-all, consider asking several students or staff members to tell a story. Stories can include things like miraculous events, natural disasters, fires, car or bike accidents, etc. If you decide to prepare beforehand, try to find a variety of stories—not three about car accidents.

Also, take note of the time it takes for students to tell their stories. Make sure everyone has an opportunity to share. And make sure you go first as an example. Your story should be very short—one minute, max. You may want to give a flicker warning before turning off your light to signal to the student that his or her turn is over.

etc.) Once they heard the news, the entire neighborhood rushed to the lake. The crowd gathered around Jesus and saw the man who had been possessed by the demons. He was sitting there, dressed normally and acting completely sane. Even so, everyone was afraid. The crowd freaked out and began to plead with Jesus to go away and leave them alone… *(cue #10: ad lib, "Please, please go away. We don't want you to ruin our other herds, too." etc.)*

So he did. As he was getting into the boat, the man said to Jesus… *(cue #11: "Please, please, Jesus. Can't I go with you?").*

Jesus replied… *(cue #12: "Don't go with me. Go home to your family, and tell them everything the Lord has done for you and how merciful he has been.")* So the man went off to visit 10 towns, all the while telling everyone what had happened to him… *(cue #13: "Hey, everyone! Remember me? I was that naked guy in the cemetery. I'd rip off the chains that bound me. I was a disgrace, but Jesus healed me! He cast out the thousands of demons inside me. I am healed and whole now.")*

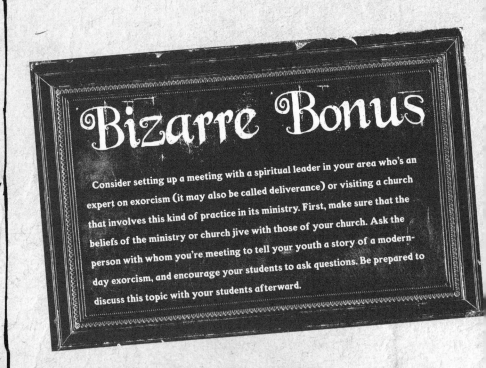

Bizarre Bonus

Consider setting up a meeting with a spiritual leader in your area who's an expert on exorcism (it may also be called deliverance) or visiting a church that involves this kind of practice in its ministry. First, make sure that the beliefs of the ministry or church jive with those of your church. Ask the person with whom you're meeting to tell your youth a story of a modern-day exorcism, and encourage your students to ask questions. Be prepared to discuss this topic with your students afterward.

MEDIA INFUSION
(optional)

Listen to the song "Cast It at the Setting Sail" from Danielson's *Ships* album. After you have listened to it, discuss the following questions.

ASK • What do you think "setting sail" represents?

• What do you think this line means: "Destroy gods and devils/and fine statues of men/ but don't throw these in the air/ or in the sea / let them be/ thrown at the setting sail/ of sweet victory"?

• What would you throw at the setting sail?

• Jesus and God aren't directly mentioned in this song, but how is their presence felt through what's being said?

• Do you find these lyrics comforting? Why or why not?

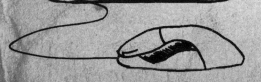

In this activity, students will [find correlations between the demoniac's situation and their own.] Distribute the four bowls of items (fabric scraps, band-aids, rocks, and paper clips). Instruct each student to take one of each item.

SAY OK. We've heard the story about the demoniac in the caves. Now, we're going to examine how it directly relates to our own lives and relationships with Jesus. You all have four small items that can remind us of this man's situation. He was unclothed. He hurt himself. He lived among the caves. He broke any restraints put on him.

And Jesus healed him with his power. When the people returned, the man was sitting calmly, fully clothed. The text is funny here, because right after it describes how the man was sitting calmly, it notes that the people were afraid. They were not afraid of the man; they were afraid of Jesus and his power.

I am going to ask some questions for you to think about silently on your own.

SAY Look at the fabric scrap. In what ways are you "unclothed"? In Jesus' time, nakedness was a sign of shame. How do you feel shame? How can Jesus heal your shame?

➡ *Give students time to think about these questions silently.*

ASK · Hold the band-aid. How are you wounded? How have you wounded yourself? How can Jesus heal your wounds? If you want to, you may put the band-aid on yourself to represent wounds.

➡ *Give students time to think about these questions silently.*

pit·tip

If you're a first-time Danielson listener, the cacophony may take a bit to get used to! However, the texts are rich with meaning. If you find it difficult to understand the lyrics at first, look for them on the Internet or read along in the liner notes.

You might have your students dig deeper into the Bible to explore more passages about demons. Have the group form smaller groups of three to five, and provide each group with one concordance and Bibles. Explain to them how a concordance works, then direct the groups to look up words such as "evil spirits," "demons," and "demon-possession." Each group can select two to four passages to read. You can choose to discuss the "Cleaning Up" questions afterward.

Perhaps you have a large class and very limited resources—that's OK. You may be able to borrow concordances from local libraries, your pastor, church staff, or others in the congregation. Also, many Bibles these days have abridged concordances in the back. Students can also flip through their Bibles to look for passages that deal with these issues. Sometimes simply paging through the Bible is a great way to find new stories.

If you prefer not to use concordances, simply have students look up Matthew 12:22-37 and John 7:10-24.

· **Hold the stone. This represents the caves the man lived among. How is death present in your life? Do you focus on death? How can Jesus remind you of our hope for the future?**

➜ *Give students time to think about these questions silently.*

· **Hold the paperclip. This represents the broken shackles. How do you break boundaries that have been set for you? How can Jesus give you new boundaries?**

➜ *Give students time to think about these questions silently.*

The Gel...

SAY We've looked at four different aspects of our lives that Jesus can heal. Now, choose one particular aspect to focus on this week. Please take the object that symbolizes this aspect...either the fabric, bandage, rock, or paper clip.

➜ *Instruct students to meet in groups of two and share their objects with one another, then pray a brief prayer together for Christ's healing power in this area of their lives. Once students have shared with one another, gather for a group prayer. Distribute the hymn handout (p. 90).*

SAY Let's pray together. For our prayer, we're going to sing (or say together) the classic hymn, "All Hail the Power of Jesus' Name." The lyrics for the hymn are on your handout. Some of the lyrics may be unfamiliar to you; there's a little glossary so you know what you're singing!

CLEANING UP

Here are some additional open-ended, thought-provoking questions. Use all or some of them to complement—or even replace—the debriefing questions for any of the activities in this study. You can guide students through this section all together, or form smaller discussion groups for more intimate dialogue.

- **In what ways did Jesus heal the Geresene man?**

- **Do you think much about the invisible powers that surround us? Why or why not? If yes, what do you think about?**

- **What do we learn about demons from today's Bible passage?**

- **What do we learn about God's attitude towards demonic forces?**

- **What other Scripture passages do you know that touch on this same topic of demon possession?**

- **What are the differences between Jesus' power and the power of the evil spirits?**

Old Hymns = Boring? They don't have to; not if *you* show some excitement about them. Old hymns can be a great introduction to Christian history and basic theology. If you're unfamiliar with "All Hail the Power of Jesus' Name," visit www.cyberhymnal .org. You can look up hundreds of public domain hymns, listen to their melodies, and read about the Christians who wrote them. To update the sound of this hymn, sing it with a slightly syncopated rhythm and clap along. If you have a youth group worship team, have them learn the hymn beforehand and lead the group in singing it.

· Do you think we see demonic activity today? Explain.

· When do you forget that Jesus is in control?

· How could Jesus help heal your life?

· How can we encourage one another not to forget Christ's power?

Mixing It Up

1 Samuel 16:14-23
(music soothes the Saul)

Mark 1:21-28
(shrieking spirits)

Mark 9:14-29
(Jesus heals a possessed boy)

"There is no need to despair; hundreds of these adult converts have been reclaimed after a brief sojourn in the Enemy's camp and are now with us. All the *habits* of the patient, both mental and bodily, are still in our favour."
—C.S. Lewis, *The Screwtape Letters* (Here, the demon Uncle Screwtape is advising Wormwood about his patient, who has recently become a Christian. Since it is a demon speaking, the "Enemy" is God.)

BELIEVE IT OR NOT

Demon possession did not end with the completion of the New Testament. It still happens today all over the world.

In a collection of stories told by missionary Christy Wilson, Wilson tells a story about a Californian who bought her family a Ouija board for Christmas. The Ouija board began, in the Lord's name, to tell the woman what to do. It told her to sell her home, leave her husband, and take her four teenage children with her to be a missionary in Afghanistan. She obeyed. It was in Afghanistan that Mr. Wilson met her. She had run out of food and the VW bus she had purchased had no battery and would not start (even though the Ouija board said it would).

At first, Mr. Wilson did not know that the woman was receiving instructions through a Ouija board, so when the bus did not start, she said, "I'm not sure this is the Lord speaking to me after all."

"How does the Lord speak to you?" Mr. Wilson asked.

When the woman told him it was a Ouija board, Mr. Wilson immediately helped her burn the board in the fireplace. The next day, another missionary joined Mr. Wilson at the woman's home, where things had gotten worse. "Whenever we would look at the sofa, it would sink down as if someone were sitting on it, although no one was around," the woman told them. The whole family had stayed awake and afraid all night.

Under the direction of Mrs. Mitchell, the group joined hands in a circle and sang "Praise God From Whom All Blessings Flow." Then, Mr. Wilson led in prayer. When he began to pray, the woman fell down on the floor inside the circle. Mrs. Mitchell pointed her finger at the woman and said, "In the name of Jesus Christ, come out! In the name of Jesus Christ, come out, and don't enter her or anyone else again!"

The woman got up and said, "A demon just came out of me." She and her family returned to the United States, and she was reconciled with her husband.

All Hail the Power of Jesus' Name

words by Edward Perronet (1726-1792)

All hail the power of Jesus' Name! Let angels prostrate fall;
Bring forth the royal diadem, and crown Him Lord of all. *(Repeat this line.)*

Sinners, whose love can ne'er forget the wormwood and the gall,
Go spread your trophies at His feet, and crown Him Lord of all. *(Repeat.)*

Let every tribe and every tongue before Him prostrate fall
And shout in universal song the crownèd Lord of all. *(Repeat.)*

O that, with yonder sacred throng, we at His feet may fall,
Join in the everlasting song, and crown Him Lord of all. *(Repeat.)*

Huh? What's this mean?

PROSTRATE: to lie facedown in adoration and submission

DIADEM: crown

WORMWOOD AND GALL: idiomatic expression for bitter life experiences

THRONG: crowd of people

DIALOGUE

LINE DIRECTIONS:

Normal: one person reads it.

Bold: 2-3 people read it simultaneously.

Bold Italics: 2-3 people ad. lib. using the lines as a starting idea.

1. Come out of this man, you evil spirit!

2. Why are you interfering with me, Jesus, Son of the Most High God? In the name of God, I beg you, don't torture me!

3. What is your name?

4. **My name is Legion because there are many of us inside this man.**

5. **Ad. Lib: *Please, please don't send us away! I want to stay right here. I hate to travel. I love living in the graveyard. Please!***

6. OK. Be gone from this man. Go into the pigs if you wish.

7. **Ad. Lib: *raucous pig sounds***

8. **Ad. Lib: *drowning pig sounds***

9. **Ad. Lib: *We lost our pigs! Demons went into them and then the pigs drowned! What are we going to do for work now?"***

10. **Ad. Lib: *Please, please go away. We don't want you to ruin our other herds, too.***

11. Please, please, Jesus. Can't I go with you?

12. Don't go with me. Go home to your family, and tell them everything the Lord has done for you and how merciful he has been.

13. Hey everyone! Remember me? I was that naked guy in the cemetery. I'd rip off the chains that bound me. I was a disgrace, but Jesus healed me! He cast out the thousands of demons inside me. I am healed and whole now.

Ear Today, Gone Tomorrow

(Jesus Re-Attaches a Severed Ear)

BIBLE STORY: LUKE 22:39-51

❧ ~ ☙

THEME: JESUS' COMPASSION

Subtopics: Revenge, Mercy, Forgiveness, Courage

Students will see how Christ showed compassion to someone who was intent on hurting him. They'll be challenged to look for ways to show kindness, even to their enemies.

SUPPLIES NEEDED:
- at least 20 cotton swabs for every student
- a straw for each student
- two big bowls
- masking tape
- water
- Bibles
- yellow food dye
- pencils
- foam cups (one for every two or three students)
- letter-sized copy paper or poster board
- a dollar bill
- your keys
- a Kleenex box
- a pair of glasses
- (optional) DVD player, TV, and the movie *The End of the Spear*

PREPARATION AND SETUP:

- In a bowl, mix several drops of yellow food coloring with a ¼ cup of water. Dip half of your cotton swabs in the yellow dye to make them look used and pukey.
- Put the yellow "ear wax" cotton swabs into a large bowl.
- Put the clean white cotton swabs into a separate bowl.

- Place two lines of masking tape on the floor a few feet apart.
- Make a photocopy of the drama handout (p. 100), one for every student.
- (optional) Set up the DVD player and TV, and cue *The End of the Spear* to chapter 14 at 1:03:14. It begins with a shot of a monkey in a tree. You'll stop the DVD at 1:10:00 as bags are being picked up to carry into the village.

Say "hey" to teenagers as they arrive. For a fun icebreaker as people trickle in, have everyone write on an index card or slip of paper the grossest thing that has ever happened to them. Be sure they don't write their name on their card. Collect them, mix them, and redistribute. Give everybody two minutes to guess the cards' rightful owners.

Continue by asking everyone to pair up. Give a straw to every person and place the two big bowls of cotton swabs in the center of the room. One bowl contains clean cotton swabs. The other bowl contains cotton swabs you have dipped in yellow dye so they look ear-waxy.

Have students form two lines, so all partners are facing each other a few feet apart.

SAY In this game of Cotton Swab Bombardment, the people in this line (designate a line) will run to the cotton swab bowls, take one cotton swab from either bowl, and shoot it through their straw at their partner. The partner should tally up the number of "hits." It is OK to move some in order to be "hit" by a partner's flying missile, just make sure you don't cross the line at your feet. After shooting a cotton swab, race as fast as you can to get another one from the bowl to shoot at your partner. I'll stop you after three minutes.

→ *Begin the game with a starting cue, and stop everyone after three minutes to ask for a report about how many times people were hit. Then give partners a chance to retaliate. Instead of grabbing cotton swabs from a bowl, just let them gather them up one by one from the floor, return to the line, and let 'em fly. Again, their partners should keep an accurate count of how many times they are hit. After three minutes, stop the game, and have pairs tabulate their grand totals. (A convoluted awards ceremony complete with trophies and the national anthem is a must.)*

pit·tip

At the end of Cotton Swab Bombardment, have students help you quickly gather up all the swabs on the floor and put them back in the bowls. You'll use them later in the study.

ASK · **When reaching for cotton swab artillery, did you grab for gross swabs or clean ones to assail your partner? Why?**

· **For those of you who went second, which swabs did you reach for?**

· **Which was the more "compassionate" choice?**

· **What do you think it means to be compassionate?**

SAY In our game, you had a split second to decide whether or not to show mercy to someone by pummeling them with clean cotton swabs instead of gross ones. We make choices like that every day. While most of our acts of mercy won't have anything to do with ear disgustingness, we're going to look at one Bible story that does.

BELIEVE IT OR NOT
In Bangladesh, a teacher was found guilty of cutting 17 of his students' ears with a pair of scissors to discipline them. Relatives of the school children rushed in and beat the teacher with sticks, and he was fired. Better off sticking with detention!

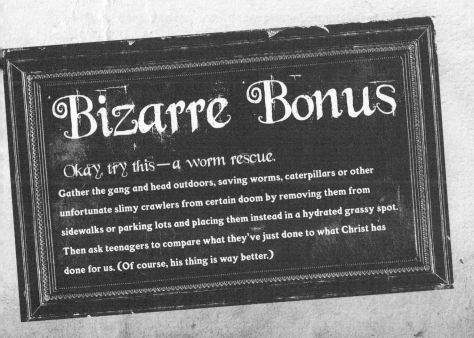

Bizarre Bonus

Okay, try this—a worm rescue.
Gather the gang and head outdoors, saving worms, caterpillars or other unfortunate slimy crawlers from certain doom by removing them from sidewalks or parking lots and placing them instead in a hydrated grassy spot. Then ask teenagers to compare what they've just done to what Christ has done for us. (Of course, his thing is way better.)

Make photocopies of the melodrama on page 100. Distribute them to your teenagers. Assign parts and have students act out what you read. At the end of the melodrama, ask students to turn to Luke 22:39-51. Have volunteers read the verses aloud for a slightly more reverent account of Christ's compassion.

ASK · What are some good reasons Jesus might have overlooked Malchus' ear debacle?

· How would you have handled the situation if you were Peter? Malchus? Jesus?

→ *Have the students team up with a partner or two and come up with a different ending to the Bible story. After a few minutes, have volunteers share what they came up with and spend a few minutes contemplating the consequences that would have followed their made-up endings.*

SAY Showing compassion to someone who is about to haul you in and execute you for crimes you didn't commit doesn't come naturally, for sure. But Jesus always did have a long-standing habit of showing mercy to undeserving people.

I think part of Jesus' appeal to the masses was his crazy love for horrifyingly depraved sickos. The more miserable the better. Bring on the big fat heathen, the deformed and contagious. He had a come-passion. "Come to me if you are sick, depressed, or just really, really messed up. I can fix that." He touched lepers, he ate with the scandalous. He reattached gooey, oozing, chopped-off ears. Sometimes compassion is the only thing that can possibly make things right.

Christ in his compassion saw that we were cut off from God. He knew the trouble we were in for and healed our souls, making a way for us to be cool with God again, even though we are as hopelessly messed up as we can be. If you don't know about that, please let me fill you in after our meeting.

> "The truth is, as believers, we've been called to help…people. We should be asking how we can use the gifts we've been given to go to all the world and live out the message of the Gospel."
>
> —Cliff Young, of the band Caedmon's Call

ASK · How has Jesus shown compassion on you when you didn't deserve it? What was your response?

· How have you shown compassion to others?

 **Give each student a piece of blank copy paper or have them work together in groups of two or three, giving each group a** bigger piece of paper (maybe poster board). See that each person (or group) gets a foam cup with food dye (yellow or other color) mixed with a small bit of water. Distribute cotton swabs.

SAY Use the cotton swabs to paint pictures of times in your own life when you've had an opportunity to show compassion to somebody. If you aren't really into painting pretty pictures with imaginary earwax, just make symbols or write words that represent these times.

➡ *They might want pencils to help them create their pictures as well. Give them several minutes to work, and when it seems like they have had enough time, ask volunteers to share their pictures with the class. Have them partner up and discuss these questions as you prompt them. Pause to give them a minute or two to answer each one.*

ASK · What can I do to be a more compassionate person?

· Who are some people in my life in need of compassion?

· How are you going to help and encourage me to follow Jesus' example of compassion?

MEDIA INFUSION (optional)

The movie *The End of the Spear* depicts the true story of five missionaries who are speared to death by the Waodani tribe in Ecuador. Instead of seeking revenge or harboring hatred, the now widowed and fatherless missionary families continued to love, pray for, seek, and minister to the violent tribe. Watch a clip beginning in chapter 14 at 1:03:14. It starts with a shot of a monkey in a tree. A narrator says, "If they would not have been women they would have been killed…" In this scene, a native girl who ran away years ago to the foreigners returns with Elisabeth Elliot, her daughter, and Rachel Saint to tell the men who speared the missionaries about God's ("Wyangongi") forgiveness. Stop the DVD at 1:10:00 as bags are being picked up to carry into the village.

There are some bare bottoms and things, so check the scene out beforehand to make sure that isn't a problem for your group. And be sure to have the subtitle feature of your TV/DVD player turned on.

SAY This batch of missionary boys made a forever impact by *(continued next page)*

following Christ's example of mercy and sacrifice. Even though it didn't go great at first, the compassion of the men's families, and the message of their love, reached the hardest hearts and transformed an entire people group.

ASK • How does this scene show us how compassion can change someone's heart?

The Gel...

Give your students three tangible, though somewhat terrifying, ideas of things they can do to show more compassion to the people around them:

- Befriend a loner at school.
- Get involved with a local charity.
- Sponsor a child overseas (see pit·tip).
- Visit church shut-ins.
- Really listen to the problems of someone who is depressed.
- Ask a single parent in our church if there is anything you can do to make his or her life easier.

pit·tip

Compassion International is a reputable organization established years ago to sponsor children worldwide who've been ravaged by extreme poverty. For a modest amount every month, just about anyone can afford to buy food and an education for a child abroad. Introduce your teenagers to the idea by showing them the Web site at www.compassion.com. Challenge students to sponsor a child, either individually or in groups. This is one really powerful way a teenager can make a global difference.

→ *Pass a cup of water around the circle. As it is passed, ask teenagers to silently pray for those who don't have enough to eat or drink.*

Then, pass your key ring around the circle. Ask your teenagers to pray for those who have no home and no means of getting from here to there.

Next, pass around a bill from your wallet or purse. Ask teenagers to pray for those families who can't make ends meet.

Then, pass around a tissue, and pray for those who are sick or hurting.

Finally, pass around a pair of glasses, and pray aloud for eyes to see the needs of those around us—and compassion to act on those needs.

BEGIN CLEANING UP

CLEANING UP

Here are some additional open-ended, thought-provoking questions. Use all or some of them to complement—or even replace—the debriefing questions for any of the activities in this study. You can guide students through this section all together, or form smaller discussion groups for more intimate dialogue.

- **How would you rate this story on a grossness scale of one to ten?**

- **If you were writing a profound, succinct, one-sentence plot summary of the made-for-TV movie version of this Bible story, how would it go?**

- **How would you define "extreme compassion?"**

- **Tell about a time when someone had compassion on you.**

- **Give three examples of opportunities you've had to show compassion.**

- **How is compassion related to mercy and forgiveness?**

- **How does compassion change people's lives?**

- **Think big—what impact can acts of compassion have on an international scale?**

- **Name one thing you can do starting today to be a more compassionate person.**

- **How do you feel about people in need? How does that compare to how God feels about people in need?**

pit·tip

Here's an idea: distribute copies of the "Cleaning Up" questions to each student. Have teenagers spread out all over the room. At the signal, have them race to pair up and ask and answer one question in one minute's time. When the timer goes off, switch partners and ask a new question. Keep it going until they've had a chance to ask and answer most of the questions.

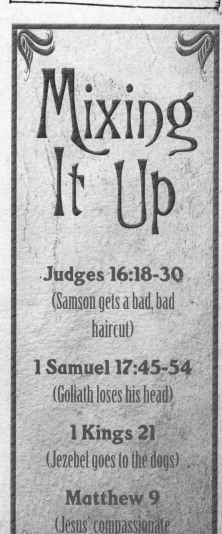

Mixing It Up

Judges 16:18-30
(Samson gets a bad, bad haircut)

1 Samuel 17:45-54
(Goliath loses his head)

1 Kings 21
(Jezebel goes to the dogs)

Matthew 9
(Jesus' compassionate healing)

MELODRAMA

CAST: JESUS, PETER, MALCHUS, A STONE, A REFEREE, SOME DISCIPLES, SOME SOLDIERS

Jesus and his disciples were walking to the Garden of Gethsemane. The disciples were fighting…shoving…poking…doing invasive wrestling maneuvers…quarreling about who would bear the title of "Disciple of Supreme Awesomeness."

When they got to the garden, Jesus took Peter and three other disciples with him and left the others to perfect their moonwalk and robot dance moves.

The four disciples dozed off as Jesus went to pray. They snored loudly. They walked around in their sleep. They unknowingly told their deepest secrets to everyone (including who they are planning to take to the next school dance).

Meanwhile, Jesus went to a nearby stone to pray. He was upset. He sobbed. He beat his fist on the stone repeatedly. Then, he awoke his disciples with his best annoying alarm-clock imitation.

The disciples were still yawning and stretching when soldiers appeared, making nasty villainous faces and waving their imaginary weaponry in the air.

Judas, who had drawn a fake and sinister mustache on his face with a semi-permanent marker, puckered up…and gave Jesus a kiss. The soldiers moved in…and their jaws dropped in wonder as Jesus spoke to them. "Betrayed with a kiss…Am I a revolutionary that you'd bring swords? Why not in the temple; why in the darkness? This is the time when the power of darkness reigns."

Peter, swashbuckling with an invisible sword, cut off one soldier's ear (Malchus) and then inspected it for earwax. Malchus let out an earthshaking wail that sounded a lot like a Celine Dion song.

Even though this soldier had violently come to arrest Jesus, Jesus had compassion on him. Jesus scolded Peter…fixed the guy's ear…and the three men embraced in a touching group hug.

A referee who was displaced after accepting a ride from a stranger in a time machine broke up the huddle, and the soldiers carried Jesus away to prison, making the sound of horse feet with their tongues. Then they cheered wildly, indicating the story was ending.

Blind-Sight-ed

(Jesus Uses Mud to Heal)

BIBLE STORY: JOHN 9:1-41

THEME: GOD'S HEALING TOUCH

Subtopics: God's Plans, Sight, Pharisees, Family, Jesus, Patience, Hope

Students will find out how Jesus unexpectedly healed a man who had been born blind. They'll better understand how God can heal their hurts and draw them closer to him.

SUPPLIES NEEDED:
- a blindfold for every two people
- approximately ¼ cup tapioca pudding for every four students
- approximately one dried bean for every four students
- bowls for about half the students you expect
- Bibles
- a roll of paper towels (for quick clean up at stations)
- two cinderblocks (see note)
- one 4'x6' plank (see note)
- a blender
- a pitcher of limeade
- small cups

continued on next page

- gummy worms
- vegetable oil
- a small bowl of dirt and a separate clear bowl of dirt

- a bucket of water
- a towel
- a paint mixing stick (or wooden spoon)
- (optional) computer(s) with Internet connection

A NOTE ABOUT THE CINDERBLOCKS AND PLANK:

Cinderblocks and a 4'x6' plank should be easily (and inexpensively) available at most home improvement stores. However, if you have a wide staircase near your meeting room that would not be easily recognized by blindfolded students as a stair, use it. The idea is to give students the feeling of walking the plank without the danger of being up too high.

PREPARATION AND SETUP:

- Arrange station supplies together: pudding, beans, bowls, and paper towels; cinderblocks and plank; blender, limeade, and cups; gummy worms, oil, and paper towels. Make sure to keep all station supplies out of students' sight.
- Make a copy of the script (pp. 109-110) for every student.

- Put some dirt in a small bowl and more in a clear bowl. Put water in a bucket.
- Gather table lamps and place them near outlets around the edge of the room and at the two stations (optional).

When students are blindfolded, turn out the overhead lights, and turn on a few lamps at the corners of the room and at the two stations. The added darkness will enhance the feeling of blindness.

The Goo...

Ask students to find a partner and choose who will go first as you distribute a blindfold to each pair.

SAY In just a moment, the person going first will put on a blindfold with their partner's help. Then your partner will walk you around, helping you get used to not being able to see. After a minute or so, your partner will ask you to choose Option A or Option B—and then guide you to that experience. I'm not going to give you any hints about the options, except to say that the two choices this time will be different from the two choices next time. To keep up the suspense for others who will share the same experience, be as quiet as possible until I ask you to remove your blindfold. And guides: I think it goes without saying that you should not give away any of the options!

➡ *Instruct guides to lead their partners around the room, allowing for a few people at each station at a time.*

Option A1: Place one dried bean in a small bowl of tapioca pudding. For sanitary reasons, give each student their own bowl of pudding; about ¼ cup per person should be sufficient. As students arrive at this option whisper that their task is to use their fingers to find the "nugget" in the bowl of snot. Have paper towels available for quick cleanup.

Option B1: As each student arrives at this station, turn on the blender briefly, then turn it off again and pour some limeade into a small cup. Whisper that they need to plug their nose and down the poison punch.

When the first group has completed their experience, turn on the lights and ask formerly blind students to blindfold former guides. Repeat the experience with two new options:

Option A2: Put two cinderblocks on the floor, and place a 4′x6′ plank on top of them. At this option students will walk the plank.

Option B2: As each student arrives at this station, put three gummy worms and ½ teaspoon of vegetable oil in a bowl. Swish the worms around so they are coated and slippery. Whisper that students have to pick up and eat the contents of their bowl. Have paper towels available for quick cleanup.

When the second group has completed their experience, turn on the lights and ask students to be seated.

ASK · **What feelings did you experience during this activity? What evoked those feelings?**

· **What did you expect from this experience?**

· **How was this activity like or unlike what you expected?**

· **What do you think it would be like to be blind?**

· **Now that you have been "restored" to sight what can you better appreciate about seeing?**

SAY While being blind might be scary sometimes, experiencing an unexpected healing might be even scarier. That's the gist of the story we're going to look at today from John 9.

BELIEVE IT OR NOT

The international Bog Snorkelling competition is held every August in the outskirts of the smallest town in Britain, Llanwrtyd Wells, in Wales. In 2006 over 100 participants gathered to complete two 60-yard laps through the disgustingly-dirty, peat moss-sludgy, creepy creature-filled Waen Rhydd bog. Competitors wear snorkels and flippers and (hopefully!) wet suits and make their way through the muck without using any conventional swimming strokes for the fastest time. People came from around the world—including Russia, Australia, and New Zealand—to compete.

Other bog snorkeling events include mountain bike bog snorkeling and a bog snorkeling triathlon. All proceeds from the events go to charity.

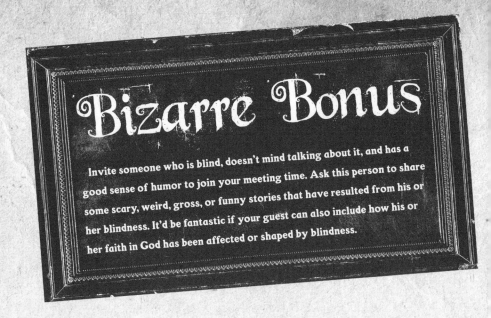

Bizarre Bonus

Invite someone who is blind, doesn't mind talking about it, and has a good sense of humor to join your meeting time. Ask this person to share some scary, weird, gross, or funny stories that have resulted from his or her blindness. It'd be fantastic if your guest can also include how his or her faith in God has been affected or shaped by blindness.

The Guts...

Ask partners to move to opposite sides of the room, and invite one courageous person from each group to read the parts of Jesus and The Man (who was born blind). Set up the room so the two groups sit facing each other and Jesus and The Man stand at either end facing each other (together, the two groups, Jesus, and The Man will form a rectangle). Assign parts to each group equally, so that one disciple, one neighbor, one parent, and one or two Pharisees are seated on each side. You can read the part of the Narrator.

Pull Jesus and The Man aside and explain that, when it arises in the script, they will enter the center of the group. Jesus will make mud (by adding a small amount of water to the small bowl of dirt—Jesus can certainly pretend to spit!) and then smear it above The Man's eyebrows. Make sure both are willing to fully play their parts.

pit·tip

Ideally, everyone will be involved in the reading of this script. If you have a larger group, assign more than one person to play each disciple, neighbor, and Pharisee, and instruct them to read in unison. If you have a smaller group, assign more than one part to each person in the two groups.

➡ *Distribute copies of the script (pp. 109-110). Tell students that this script will be more fun if they really pay attention and jump in to deliver their lines. Read it together.*

ASK · What did you notice about people's responses to this healing?

· How do you think you'd have responded if you'd been The Man?

➡ *Distribute Bibles as students form small groups. Ask them to read Psalm 40:5 and Romans 12:12 and discuss these questions:*

ASK · How would you describe the healing in the story of Jesus and The Blind Man? Why do you think Jesus chose to heal in this way—when he could have done it in any way?

· Have you ever seen someone healed by God? How has God healed pains in your life—physical, emotional, or spiritual? Explain.

· Why is God's plan for healing sometimes uncomfortable? unexpected? strange?

· What might be God's multiple purposes in healing us?

· What impact does God have on your life? relationships with others? relationship with Jesus?

· How can you be glad for all of God's healing, even when it's unexpected or even unpleasant? What does that have to do with being patient in trouble and always prayerful?

➡ *Allow each group to share at least one interesting thing they discussed.*

SAY God cares about each of us, and he wants to heal us for his purpose and in his perfect timing. Thing is, God's healing—and his plans in general—often come in very unexpected ways. I mean, nobody would imagine Jesus would use spit to heal a blind man.

But God has a long history of surprising people. Case in point: God's people, the Jews, waited for and longed for their Messiah for centuries. They anticipated a king who would take political control and create peace for them as a nation. The baby born in a Bethlehem manger who refused political involvement and died on a cross…well, that was too unexpected for them to understand as a fulfillment of God's plans and a miracle in their midst. Galatians 1:4-5 says, "(He) gave himself for our sins to rescue us from the present evil age, according to the will of our God and Father, to whom be glory for ever and ever."

The great news is, through this highly unexpected plan for salvation, God also designed a healing for our broken relationship with him. This is the ultimate healing. When we make a faith commitment to Jesus, that relationship is made whole, and we know we will be with Jesus forever. And even though it can be surprising and maybe a little scary, it's not gross at all (no spit involved).

MEDIA INFUSION (optional)

With your students, go online and find stories of people being healed by God or through the power of prayer. (You can easily find surprising stories of healing by typing key words such as "healing prayer" into an Internet search engine. Read a few of these stories together. Then discuss:

• **What do you think is remarkable or surprising about these stories?**

• **How might God's healing be better than what we expect?**

The Grit...

While students watch, add water to dirt and mix up a batch of mud.

SAY Jesus' plans in today's story included restoring sight to The Blind Man, but Jesus also wanted others to witness God's power at work. In another situation, God's plan might not have included restoring sight but wanting The Blind Man to remain blind in order to trust God more.

You see, sometimes we can easily recognize God's touch on our lives, and sometimes it's fun and wonderful; other times what God is doing may seem scary, strange, and hard to deal with. Nevertheless, God's healing touch always accomplishes his perfect purpose, even when our expectations aren't met. Ephesians 3:20-21 says, "Now to him who is able to do immeasurably more than all we ask or imagine, according to his power that is at work within us, to him be the glory in the church and in Christ Jesus throughout all generations, for ever and ever! Amen."

➡️ *Ask students to think of one example of God's healing, including emotional, mental, relational, and spiritual. Go around the room and let each person share. After each person shares their example, say in unison,*

"Now glory be to God!"

When everyone has shared, invite students to close their eyes and hold their hands open in front of them.

SAY Thank you for sharing. God is a terrifically powerful God! Now, I want you to think about your life. Think about a hurt you're experiencing this week, this month, this year, into the future...Imagine you are holding this hurt in your hands. Can you hold your plans open to God and accept that God might want to heal you, even if his healing may not look the way you expect it to? *Pause.* Are you ready to accept God's touch on your life, whatever it may be? *Pause.*

The Gel...

When they're ready, invite students to come up and put some mud somewhere on their body. This is as a sign of their readiness to give their hurts to God and trust in his healing power.

Encourage students that, like The Blind Man washing in the pool of Siloam, they can commit to doing what God says every morning and night as they wash their face.

"Amazing grace! How sweet the sound That saved a wretch like me! I once was lost, but now am found; Was blind, but now I see."

BEGIN CLEANING UP

Scary, Gross & Weird STORIES from the Bible

CLEANING UP

Here are some additional open-ended, thought-provoking questions. Use all or some of them to complement—or even replace—the debriefing questions for any of the activities in this study. You can guide students through this section all together, or form smaller discussion groups for more intimate dialogue.

- The disciples thought disability was a result of sin. What's your take on this? What might God think of this idea?
- In this story, Jesus said we must quickly carry out the tasks God has given us. What tasks do you think God intends you to do?
- Why is Jesus' healing sometimes uncomfortable? How can you explain what seems to be a paradox?
- What do you think Jesus means that he is the light of the world? How would you explain this to someone else?
- Why do you think it was so hard for people to accept that Jesus healed The Blind Man?
- To which character in this story do you most relate? Why?
- In what ways were the Pharisees actually the "blind" characters?
- Has God ever pointed out a spiritual blind spot in your life? If so, how? What was that experience like?
- What might Jesus' plan to heal you include? How will you respond?

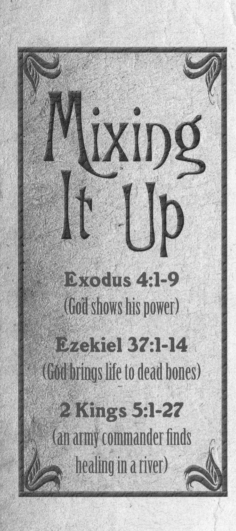

Mixing It Up

Exodus 4:1-9
(God shows his power)

Ezekiel 37:1-14
(God brings life to dead bones)

2 Kings 5:1-27
(an army commander finds healing in a river)

SCRIPT

NARRATOR: AS JESUS WAS WALKING ALONG, HE SAW A MAN WHO HAD BEEN BLIND FROM BIRTH. HIS DISCIPLES ASKED HIM...

Disciples 1 & 2: Teacher...

Disciple 1: ...why was this man born blind?

Disciple 2: Was it a result of his own sins...

Disciple 1: ... or those of his parents?

Jesus: It was not because of his sins or his parents' sins. He was born blind so the power of God could be seen in him. All of us must quickly carry out the tasks assigned us by the one who sent me, because there is little time left before the night falls and all work comes to an end. But while I am still here in the world, I am the light of the world.

NARRATOR: JESUS SPIT ON THE GROUND, MADE MUD WITH THE SALIVA, AND SMOOTHED THE MUD OVER THE BLIND MAN'S EYES.

(**Jesus** *walks into the center, make mud, and smear it above The Man's eyebrows.*)

Jesus: Go and wash in the pool of Siloam.

NARRATOR: SILOAM MEANS "SENT." SO THE MAN WENT WHERE HE WAS SENT AND WASHED, AND CAME BACK SEEING!

The Man: *(Washes face, excited and overwhelmed!)* I can see!

NARRATOR: HIS NEIGHBORS AND OTHERS WHO KNEW HIM AS A BLIND BEGGAR ASKED EACH OTHER...

Neighbor 1: Is this the same man...

Neighbor 2: ...that beggar?

Neighbor 1: No...

Neighbor 2: ...but he surely looks like him!

The Man: I am the same man!

Neighbor 2: Who healed you?

Neighbor 1: What happened?

The Man: The man they call Jesus made mud and smoothed it over my eyes and told me, 'Go to the pool of Siloam and wash off the mud.' I went and washed, and now I can see!

Neighbors 1 & 2: Where is he now?

The Man: I don't know.

NARRATOR: THEN THEY TOOK THE MAN TO THE PHARISEES. NOW AS IT HAPPENED, JESUS HAD HEALED THE MAN ON A SABBATH AND THE PHARISEES ASKED THE MAN ALL ABOUT IT.

The Man: He smoothed the mud over my eyes, and when it was washed away, I could see!

Pharisee 1: This man Jesus...

Pharisee 2: ...is not from God...

Pharisee 1: ...for he is working...

Pharisee 2: ...on the Sabbath.

Pharisee 1: But how could an ordinary sinner...

Pharisee 2: ...do such miraculous signs?

NARRATOR: SO THERE WAS A DEEP DIVISION OF OPINION AMONG THEM, AND THEY QUESTIONED HIM AGAIN.

Pharisee 1: This man who opened your eyes...

Pharisee 2: ...who do you say he is?

The Man: I think he must be a prophet.

NARRATOR: THE JEWISH LEADERS WOULDN'T BELIEVE HE HAD BEEN BLIND, SO THEY CALLED IN HIS PARENTS.

Pharisee 1: Is this your son?

Pharisee 2: Was he born blind?

Pharisees 1 & 2: If so, how can he see?

Parent 1: We know this is our son...

Parent 2: ...and that he was born blind...

Parent 1: ...but we don't know how he can see...

Parent 2: ...or who healed him.

Parent 1: He is old enough...

Parent 2: ...to speak for himself.

Parents 1 & 2: Ask him.

NARRATOR: THEY SAID THIS BECAUSE THEY WERE AFRAID OF THE JEWISH LEADERS, WHO HAD ANNOUNCED THAT ANYONE SAYING JESUS WAS THE MESSIAH WOULD BE EXPELLED FROM THE SYNAGOGUE. SO FOR THE SECOND TIME THE PHARISEES CALLED IN THE MAN WHO HAD BEEN BLIND.

Pharisee 2: Give glory to God by telling the truth...

Pharisee 1: ...because we know Jesus is a sinner.

The Man: I don't know whether he is a sinner. But I know this: I was blind, and now I can see!

Pharisee 2: But what did he do?

Pharisee 1: How did he heal you?

The Man: Look! I told you once. Didn't you listen? Why do you want to hear it again? Do you want to become his disciples, too?

NARRATOR: THEY CURSED HIM.

Pharisee 1: You are his disciple...

Pharisee 2: ...but we are disciples of Moses.

Pharisee 1: We know God spoke to Moses...

Pharisee 2: ...but as for this man...

Pharisees 1 & 2: ...we don't know anything about him.

The Man: Why, that's very strange! He healed my eyes, and yet you don't know anything about him! Well, God doesn't listen to sinners, but he is ready to hear those who worship him and do his will. Never since the world began has anyone been able to open the eyes of someone born blind. If this man were not from God, he couldn't do it.

Pharisee 2: You were born in sin!

Pharisee 1: Are you trying to teach us?

NARRATOR: AND THEY THREW HIM OUT OF THE SYNAGOGUE. JESUS HEARD WHAT HAD HAPPENED AND FOUND THE MAN.

Jesus: Do you believe in the Son of Man?

The Man: Who is he, sir, because I would like to believe in him.

Jesus: You have seen him and he is speaking to you!

The Man: Yes, Lord, I believe! *(Bow before Jesus.)*

NARRATOR: AND HE WORSHIPPED JESUS.

Jesus: I have come to judge the world. I have come to give sight to the blind and to show those who think they see that they are blind.

Pharisees 1 & 2: Are you saying we are blind?

Jesus: If you were blind, you wouldn't be guilty. But you remain guilty because you claim you can see.

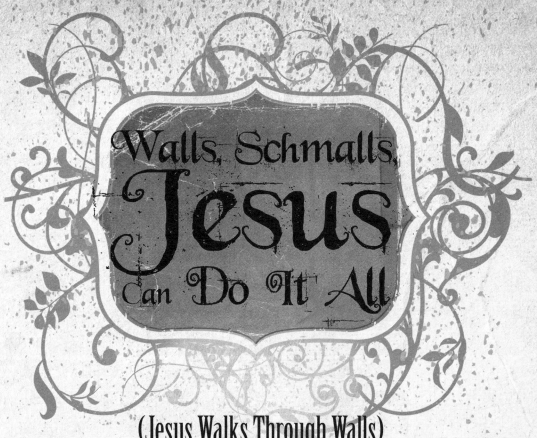

Walls, Schmalls, Jesus Can Do It All

(Jesus Walks Through Walls)

BIBLE STORY: JOHN 20:1-31

THEME: ETERNAL LIFE

Subtopics: Fear, Death, God's Power, Disciples, Following Jesus, Faith, Doubt

Jesus died, and his followers were grief-stricken. But then the unexpected happened: the risen Jesus appeared to his followers. Students will consider their thoughts and feelings about Jesus' death and resurrection—and gain a new personal understanding of eternal life and God's power to conquer death.

SUPPLIES NEEDED:
- a hat, basket, or bag
- 10 slips of paper
- one piece of gray construction paper for every two people
- masking tape

- one bandana for every four to six people
- markers
- (optional) DVD player and TV, movie *What Dreams May Come*
- Bibles

PREPARATION AND SETUP:

- Cut 8½" x 11" pieces of gray construction paper in half, and then use scissors to round the top two corners so you have a tombstone shape. You'll need one per student.
- On 10 slips of paper, write the following phobias: fear of the dark, fear of public speaking, fear of flying, fear of heights, fear of clowns, fear of snakes, fear of water, fear of failure, fear of closed spaces, and fear of open spaces. Put them in the hat, bag, or basket.

- Tape two lines on the floor about 15 feet apart. The floor must be clear to run between.
- Make a photocopy of the script (pp. 120-122) for everyone.
- (optional) Set up the TV and DVD player, and cue the movie *What Dreams May Come*. Begin the counter at 0:24:40 when Chris Nielsen (Robin Williams) first arrives in heaven and is running down a tunnel. You'll stop the clip at 0:27:00, when Chris says, "Maybe you're in mine."

The Goo... **Ask students to form groups of 10 and show them the hat, bag, or basket containing phobia slips.**

SAY Have you ever heard someone say they'd rather die than speak in public? Well, we're going to confront that fear head on! In this hat are 10 slips of paper each with the name of a common phobia, such as fear of the dark or of heights. One by one you'll come up, choose a slip of paper, and then you'll have 30 seconds to talk about this fear with your group. You can share a personal story, something that happened to a friend (keep it anonymous and clean, please), or how you think this phobia might affect someone. Here's the kicker: while you speak, you'll have two additional group members to pose and/or interact with to help you make your point about the fear.

 Make sure everyone gets a chance to speak.

pit·tip

If you have more than one group, you can have more than one hat with phobias in it—or you could stick with one hat and have all speakers speak on the same topic at the same time.

ASK · How did you feel as you waited for your turn? While you spoke?

· How did it make you feel to have to interact with other group members while you spoke? Why?

· Which of these fears hits closest to home? Why?

➡ *Give each person one paper tombstone and a pencil.*

SAY Now we're going to spend a few minutes focusing on the fear of death. Write a prayer to God about your thoughts and feelings about death. Use these questions to guide your prayer:

· **Are you afraid of death? Why or why not?**

· **What do you think will happen after you die?**

· **How do you feel about God when you think about death?**

➡ *Allow students a few quiet minutes to pray.*

SAY People have all sorts of opinions on what happens to us after death: that that's the end of us, that we become ghosts, that we come back to life in a different form, and so on. Today we're going to look at what happened after Jesus died and discover what that means for us.

pit·tip

Be extremely sensitive during this activity and adjust it to fit your students' individual needs. For instance, in advance of this study, you might want to check in with your adult leaders to see if anyone has heard of a student suffering the loss of a grandparent, friend, or even a pet.

On the other hand, depending on your group, you might take a light-hearted approach by playing creepy haunted-house style music while they pray. You could also decorate the room with gravestones and other haunted house decorations.

Bizarre Bonus

Take your group to a cemetery for a treasure hunt. See who can find:

· the oldest grave marker
· the person who lived longest
· their last name on the most grave markers
· a grave marker they think is funny
· the newest grave marker
· the person who died youngest
· the most interesting grave marker
· a grave marker they think is sad

Be sure to warn students not to walk or run over gravesites and to be respectful of the families these graves represent. Before you leave, spend a few minutes together thanking God for the gift of eternal life to those who have made a faith commitment to Jesus.

Ask students to form groups of six while you put two parallel tape lines on the floor (as long as needed for your group, but as wide apart as your meeting space will allow). Ask them to decide who will play Mary, John, Peter, two Angels, and Jesus. Mary, Peter, and John should stand on one side of one of the tape lines, while the Angels and Jesus stand facing them on the other side.

Give each Peter and John pair a bandana and ask them to tie their ankles for a three-legged race. During scenes two and three, make sure you are standing near the light switch. Also, warn the student playing Jesus to quickly pop into place while the lights are out.

SAY We're going to act out today's Bible story from John 20 in three scenes. The first scene will have half of you racing back and forth. In scenes two and three most of you will be disciples and we'll cast Jesus, Thomas, and a Narrator.

Before we begin, I want you to close your eyes and imagine the scene. Jesus has been crucified—a horrible, messy, painful death. He has been dead three days. His followers feel crushed and confused, having lost their teacher, their master, their meaning in life. Early one morning Mary goes to the tomb and finds an even-more confusing surprise…

→ *Encourage students to use the full range of their dramatic abilities to read this script. Between each scene ask the following questions:*

· **What emotions do you imagine people are experiencing in this scene? Explain.**

· **How do people respond to Jesus?**

ASK · **What unusual things did Jesus do in John 20?**

· **Why do you think people responded to Jesus the way they did?**

· **What does John 20 tell us about Jesus' resurrection? about Jesus' divinity?**

pit·tip

MEDIA INFUSION (optional)

Show a clip from the movie *What Dreams May Come,* when Chris Nielsen (Robin Williams) first arrives in heaven and is running down a tunnel. Begin the counter at 0:24:40 and conclude at 0:27:00, when Chris says, "Maybe you're in mine."

SAY This movie doesn't present a picture of heaven that's exactly like the one in the Bible, but it's a creative view of the afterlife.

ASK • What do you think might be accurate about this creative view of heaven? What's inaccurate?

• What do you think heaven looks like? What might there be to look forward to?

• Why might someone hope that heaven is like this?

• Is there anything about heaven that you think will be uncomfortable, boring or surprising? Explain.

SAY God raised Jesus from the dead, conquering sin and death. Because Jesus Christ is God, he could do things no one else could do. Let's talk now about how that impacts our lives.

The Crit...

Ask students to rejoin their drama groups as you distribute Bibles. Instruct groups to look up Psalm 40:10 and 2 Timothy 1:9-10, and discuss these questions:

- According to 2 Timothy 1:9-10, what has been God's long-time plan?

- According to these passages, what does God's power have to do with eternal life after death? How does Jesus fit into that equation?

- How do you think Jesus would explain to someone why we don't have to be afraid of death?

- How do you think and feel about this? How will your response change your life?

 Distribute markers and make sure students have their tombstones.

SAY Jesus Christ, Son of God and God himself, was born on earth, lived a holy life, died on the cross, rose from the dead, and did some incredible things, all because he loves us and wants us to live for his glory. All our fears, including those of public speaking and of death, cannot stop Jesus' love from penetrating our lives. I am going to read Romans 8:38-39 to you.

BELIEVE IT OR NOT

Dosha the dog seems to have the nine lives of a cat. In April 2003, a police officer found Dosha, a ten-month-old mixed-breed, on the side of the road near her owner's Clearwater, California, home. Dosha had been hit by a car and the police officer, in a meaningful act of mercy, shot Dosha in the head to put her out of her misery. Dosha was then put in a bright orange doggy-style body bag and into a freezer at an animal control center. Two hours later veterinarian Deborah Sally opened the freezer and found Dosha standing upright inside the bag. So even though Dosha was hit by a car, shot in the head, and then suffered hypothermia from the freezer, the vet said the "miracle girl" is doing "amazingly well."

BEGIN
CLEANING
UP

The Gel...

SAY As I read, I want you to write words or short phrases across what you wrote earlier on your tombstone to represent what you've discovered about Jesus...and how you will respond to Jesus.

Romans 8:38-39: *"For I am convinced that neither death nor life, neither angels nor demons, neither the present nor the future, nor any powers, neither height nor depth, nor anything else in all creation, will be able to separate us from the love of God that is in Christ Jesus our Lord."*

Challenge students to use the back of their tombstone to make a list of examples of God's power this week and to try to add at least three things to the list each day.

> "The Galilean
> has been too
> great for our
> small hearts."
> —H.G. Well

CLEANING UP

Here are some additional open-ended, thought-provoking questions. Use all or some of them to complement—or even replace—the debriefing questions for any of the activities in this study. You can guide students through this section all together, or form smaller discussion groups for more intimate dialogue.

- Why do you think Mary was concerned that someone took Jesus' body? How would that have affected the Christian faith?

- What was John's response when he entered the tomb? If John believed, why do you think Mary was still crying?

- When did Mary recognize Jesus? Why do you think it took that long?

- Why do you think the disciples were afraid of the Jewish leaders?

- What's the most unbelievable thing you've ever seen someone do? How does that compare with what Jesus does in John 20?

- Why do you think Jesus says to his followers, "Peace be with you"? How can we have peace when it comes to our death? to the idea of eternal life?

- What do you think about Thomas' reaction to his friends' claims to have seen Jesus: understandable, or faithless? Explain your position.

- What's your reaction to the idea of death? What impact does God's plan for eternal life have on you?

- What difference does it make to your life that Jesus rose from the dead? that Jesus is God?

- How can your friends encourage your relationship in Jesus? How will you encourage your friends' and family members' relationships with Jesus?

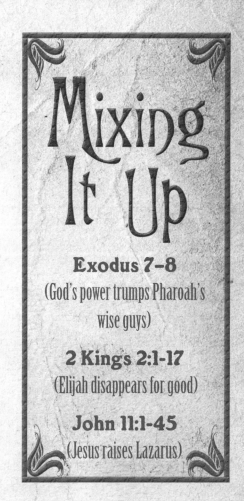

Mixing It Up

Exodus 7–8
(God's power trumps Pharoah's wise guys)

2 Kings 2:1-17
(Elijah disappears for good)

John 11:1-45
(Jesus raises Lazarus)

SCRIPT

SCENE 1

NARRATOR: EARLY SUNDAY MORNING, WHILE IT WAS STILL DARK, MARY MAGDALENE CAME TO THE TOMB AND FOUND THAT THE STONE HAD BEEN ROLLED AWAY FROM THE ENTRANCE.

(**Mary** *runs to tomb, pause, run back.*)

NARRATOR: SHE RAN AND FOUND SIMON PETER AND THE OTHER DISCIPLE, THE ONE WHOM JESUS LOVED.

Mary: They have taken the Lord's body out of the tomb, and I don't know where they have put him!

NARRATOR: PETER AND THE OTHER DISCIPLE RAN TO THE TOMB TO SEE.

(**Peter & John** *run to tomb.*)

(**Mary** *follow them.*)

NARRATOR: JOHN OUTRAN PETER AND GOT THERE FIRST. HE STOOPED AND LOOKED IN AND SAW THE LINEN CLOTH, BUT DIDN'T GO IN. THEN PETER ARRIVED AND WENT INSIDE. HE ALSO NOTICED THE LINEN WRAPPINGS LYING THERE, WHILE THE CLOTH THAT HAD COVERED JESUS' HEAD WAS FOLDED UP AND LYING TO THE SIDE. THEN JOHN ALSO WENT IN, AND HE SAW AND BELIEVED—UNTIL THEN THEY HADN'T REALIZED THAT THE SCRIPTURES SAID HE WOULD RISE FROM THE DEAD. THEN THEY WENT HOME.

(**Peter & John** *run back.*)

NARRATOR: MARY WAS STANDING OUTSIDE THE TOMB CRYING, AND AS SHE WEPT, SHE STOOPED AND LOOKED IN. SHE SAW TWO WHITE-ROBED ANGELS SITTING AT THE HEAD AND FOOT OF THE PLACE WHERE THE BODY OF JESUS HAD BEEN LYING.

Angels: Why are you crying?

Mary: Because they have taken away my Lord and I don't know where they have put him.

NARRATOR: SHE GLANCED OVER HER SHOULDER AND SAW SOMEONE STANDING BEHIND HER. IT WAS JESUS, BUT SHE DIDN'T RECOGNIZE HIM.

Jesus: Why are you crying? Who are you looking for?

NARRATOR: SHE THOUGHT HE WAS THE GARDENER.

Mary: Sir, if you have taken him away, tell me where you have put him, and I will go and get him.

Jesus: Mary!

Mary: *(Falling at his feet)* Teacher!

Jesus: Go find my brothers and tell them that I am ascending to my Father and your Father, my God and your God.

Mary: *(Run back.)*

NARRATOR: MARY MAGDALENE FOUND THE DISCIPLES.

Mary: I have seen the Lord! *(Freeze.)*

SCENE 2

NARRATOR: THAT EVENING THE DISCIPLES WERE MEETING BEHIND LOCKED DOORS BECAUSE THEY WERE AFRAID OF THE JEWISH LEADERS. SUDDENLY...

(Lights off & on)

NARRATOR: ...JESUS WAS STANDING THERE AMONG THEM!

Jesus: Peace be with you. *(Hold out your hands to them and show them your side.)*

NARRATOR: THEY WERE FILLED WITH JOY WHEN THEY SAW THEIR LORD!

Disciples: *(Shouts of joy!)*

Jesus: Peace be with you.

Disciples: *(Silence!)*

Jesus: As the Father has sent me, so I send you. *(Blow on Disciples.)* Receive the Holy Spirit. If you forgive anyone's sins, they are forgiven. If you refuse to forgive them, they are unforgiven. *(Freeze.)*

SCENE 3

NARRATOR: THOMAS WAS NOT WITH THE OTHERS WHEN JESUS CAME.

Disciples: We have seen the Lord!

Thomas: I won't believe it unless I see the nail wounds in his hands, put my fingers into them, and place my hand into the wound in his side. *(Freeze.)*

NARRATOR: EIGHT DAYS LATER THE DISCIPLES, INCLUDING THOMAS, WERE TOGETHER AGAIN. THE DOORS WERE LOCKED; BUT SUDDENLY...

(Lights off & on)

NARRATOR: ...JESUS WAS STANDING AMONG THEM.

Jesus: Peace be with you. *(To Thomas)* Put your finger here and see my hands. Put your hand into the wound in my side. Don't be faithless any longer. Believe!

Thomas: My Lord and my God! *(Fall at Jesus' feet.)*

Jesus: You believe because you have seen me. Blessed are those who haven't seen me and believe anyway.

Disciples: We saw him do many other miraculous signs besides the ones recorded in this book.

NARRATOR: BUT THESE ARE WRITTEN SO THAT YOU MAY BELIEVE THAT JESUS IS THE MESSIAH, THE SON OF GOD, AND THAT BY BELIEVING IN HIM YOU WILL HAVE LIFE.

The End (of the Bible) Is Near!

(Revelation Happenings)

BIBLE STORY: REVELATION 1:9-18

THEME: HOPE IN TIMES OF SUFFERING
Subtopics: God, End Times, Authority, Sharing Your Faith, Justice

Students will learn that the bizarre—and sometimes terrifying—imagery of God and the end of the world are not so much horrific…as hopeful.

SUPPLIES NEEDED:
- Bibles
- a box of colored pencils for every five students
- as many digital cameras as possible (one for every five students, if possible)
- a pile of magazines for every five students
- large piece of paper for every five students
- several pitchers of water
- one paper cup for every four students
- (optional) CD player, Matt Redman's *Blessed Be Your Name: The Songs of Matt Redman Vol. 1.*
- (optional) TV and DVD player, the movie *War of the Worlds*

A NOTE ON DIGITAL CAMERAS:

This might seem like a high-maintenance supply, but digital cameras are so common that you shouldn't have a problem rounding up enough for this study. Ask your students to bring their own cameras; if you still need more, send out word that you need to borrow from any willing congregation members. Of course, with any borrowed items, clearly label—and keep close tabs on—the cameras so that they're safely returned to their owners.

PREPARATION AND SETUP:

- Have several pitchers of water and enough paper cups for every group of four to have one.
- Photocopy the handout (p. 132) for each student.
- Have ready colored pencils, magazines, large pieces of paper, and digital cameras.

- (optional) Have a TV and DVD player with the movie *War of the Worlds* cued to 0:24:30 (scene five)—but be prepared to play only the sound without the video.
- (optional) Cue a CD player to the song "Blessed Be Your Name" on the album *Blessed Be Your Name: The Songs of Matt Redman Vol. 1.*

The Goo...

To heighten the effect of this activity, you can choose to have the *audio* from *War of the Worlds* playing extremely loudly when students walk in the room. Cue the DVD to 0:24:30 (scene five), but do not explain why the screen is dark. Have a digital camera, a pile of magazines, and a box of colored pencils and a large piece of paper for every five students.

SAY I've spent a lot of time studying the book of Revelation lately, and I've discovered that the numbers add up: the world will end tomorrow.

ASK · What would you do if you knew the world were literally going to end at 6:00 am tomorrow?

SAY I also know how it's going to end, but that's for me to know and you to find out (sorry, flashback to second grade). Anyway, get into groups of five and create a snapshot of how you really think the world might end. Think of it like a slide show of still photographs. Using colored pencils and/or magazine images, place images on the large sheet of paper, and take a digital photograph of your creation. Then think of what happens next and create a new image, then photograph it. For instance, the first picture could be a meteor hitting the Earth, the second one could be a tidal wave, and so on..

 Let the audio of the movie continue to play while students work. After a few minutes, turn off the sound, and have them explain their creations.

ASK · Do you think it could really happen this way, that we might get short notice of a huge catastrophe? Why or why not?

· How do events such as wars and catastrophes in the world make you feel? How much attention do you give them? Why?

· What have you heard about the book of Revelation and what it says about the end of the world?

· Do you agree or disagree with the things you've heard? Explain.

· What do you think God might have to do with the end of the world?

· Do you feel any hope when you think about the end of the world? about suffering and catastrophe? Explain.

SAY Let's look at some intriguing—and often bizarre—passages from the book of Revelation and talk about the hope we can find in darkness or suffering.

BELIEVE IT OR NOT

In the first century, the wicked Emperor Nero was willing to knock off anyone he thought might threaten his power. He's best known for beginning the early persecutions of the Christians, but a lesser known and more sinister story is how he tried to assassinate his own mother, Agrippina. Nero actually had an entire ship built that was designed to collapse at sea, giving his mom a one-way ticket to Davy Jones' locker. Sure enough, the plan worked… um,…swimmingly, except that his mom was a strong enough swimmer to make it to shore. Later Nero would dispatch his personal guard to track her down.

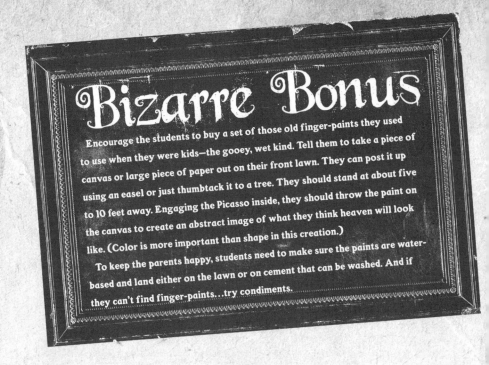

Bizarre Bonus

Encourage the students to buy a set of those old finger-paints they used to use when they were kids—the gooey, wet kind. Tell them to take a piece of canvas or large piece of paper out on their front lawn. They can post it up using an easel or just thumbtack it to a tree. They should stand at about five to 10 feet away. Engaging the Picasso inside, they should throw the paint on the canvas to create an abstract image of what they think heaven will look like. (Color is more important than shape in this creation.)

To keep the parents happy, students need to make sure the paints are water-based and land either on the lawn or on cement that can be washed. And if they can't find finger-paints…try condiments.

SAY When you first dive into the book of Revelation, you find a mess of symbols and images that don't seem to have any ties to the world you live in. Or, worse, you suddenly start watching the skies for some freakishly catastrophic events to signal the coming end of the world. Throughout history, people have made predictions about when the world would end based on the book of Revelation. It looks like predictions haven't panned out so far.

However, the most important part of Revelation is not *when* the world will come to an end, but *what happens next.*

First, you need to know a couple of things about who John was writing to and why. John was writing at the end of the first century to Christians who were being persecuted by the Romans. Emperor Nero, then on the throne, would use Christians for sport in the gladiatorial contests, even throwing them to the lions. He required everyone to pray to him. Revelation is a book that talks about God's final judgment on people who persecute the righteous. The bad guys get it in the end. So John writes to encourage them and to remind them that they come from a long line of people who stood up to bad kings.

Distribute the handout "Returning to the Lions' Den" (p. 132).

SAY In pairs, look over this sheet of paper and observe the similarities between the book of Revelation and the book of Daniel. Both Daniel and John are describing God on the throne of heaven.

 Allow a moment for students to do so.

ASK · **What do you think of this image of God?**

· **What do you think the symbols mean?**

· **Why do you think John is using the Old Testament images to describe God?**

SAY The Jews knew what it meant to be thrown into the lions' den. It had happened before, when the king of Persia threw Daniel to the lions for refusing to pray to him. Since it is happening again, John is reminding them that God is still in control when they suffer injustice. Daniel's God is still the same God in John's day, and the Christians of the first century can trust him again. Just as the king of Babylon was overthrown by God, so the emperor of Rome could be overthrown. Now let's read this passage together.

 Have a volunteer read Revelation 1:9-18 aloud for the whole group.

ASK · **What might some of these images mean?**

· **How would it feel for John's audience to be reminded of Daniel?**

· **Why is a vision of God in heaven important for people who are suffering?**

· **How might you share what you believe with someone who is suffering?**

pit·tip

Students may not relate to stories of persecution at the hands of corrupt governments (don't let it turn into a complaint about their first speeding ticket…you know, the one you kind of think they earned). But students do know what injustice is. They've been unfairly blamed and labeled, back-stabbed by friends, punished for a sibling's wrongdoing, and put in a box by a judgmental teacher. Try to draw the story of first-century suffering into their world by telling a story about your own experience as a teenager. Talk about the sense of injustice you felt. When you begin with where students currently are, they'll follow you where you're going—even if it's to a foreign country 2000 years ago.

SAY Since we've focused on the great promises that the book of Revelation gives to those who are suffering, rather than on the details of the end of the world, let's take one more look at the topic of perseverance. In Revelation, John hopes that his friends in the churches will persevere through their suffering to discover that God rewards them in the end.

 Ask a student to read Revelation 3:14-16.

ASK · Using your own words, what does God have to say to his church in this passage?

· How might you feel if you received this letter?

· Why might a suffering church have become "lukewarm in their faith"?

SAY I want to make sure you have a good (but slightly gross) visual image of what we're talking about here.

 For this little object lesson, you'll need a pitcher of water and one paper cup for every four students. This activity is best done outside or over tiled floor.

Have students form groups of four. Give each group a paper cup. Have a pitcher (or pitchers) of water available to the whole group.

SAY Have one person in your group volunteer to hold a mouthful of water in his or her mouth. Have you ever seen comedians or actors spit a spray of water out of their mouths when they're surprised? Here's your chance to test your skills. Each person in the group will take turns making an outlandish statement, like, "The other day, I sneezed so loud my intestines came out." Remember, scary, gross, and weird are completely appropriate here—within reason. When the person with the water thinks they've heard the most outlandish one...well, you know. Try to stand out of the direction of the spray!

MEDIA INFUSION
(optional)

Listen to Matt Redman's song "Blessed Be Your Name" off the album *Blessed Be Your Name: The Songs of Matt Redman Vol. 1*. Afterward, discuss the lyrics.

ASK • What did this song tell us about praising God in all situations? Do you think it's easier to do this when things are going well, or when you're hurting? Explain.

• How would you describe this song's message about suffering? hope?

• How easy or difficult is it to praise God when "there's pain in the offering"? When have you experienced this?

...nutes to play this game.

---

*...gives you an idea of how God responds to us when we're
...t on matters of faith.*

> **ASK** · **What do you think it means when God threatens
> to spit his church out of his mouth? What would be a
> real-life equivalent of this?**
>
> · **What purpose might suffering have? Why can we
> have hope in dark times and suffering?**
>
> · **How does having hope affect the way we live every
> day? the way we interact with people? with God?**
>
> · **In what ways will experiencing God's hope change
> how you go through tough times?**

→ *Gather everyone in the group in a circle (or for larger groups, in
circles of ten to fifteen). Place an empty chair in the center of the circle.*

SAY We have to admit that we don't know what God looks like. In the
book of Revelation, John uses all kinds of symbols to describe God, but
they just point towards ideas about God. We can't really imagine him
physically, although we can kind of imagine what Jesus might look like.
We're going to pray using a prayer in Revelation. Imagine that the chair in
the center of the circle is a throne. Picture Jesus sitting on the throne.

> "I don't need to be
> made to look evil.
> I can do that on
> my own."
> —Christopher Walken

BEGIN
CLEANING
UP

The Gel...

SAY Each person in the circle can name either a reason you have hope or a reason you're thankful. This can be a word or a sentence. After someone shares, I'll say aloud: "You are worthy, O Lord our God, to receive glory and honor and power. For you created all things, and they exist because you created what you pleased." Once you get the hang of this, please feel free to say this along with me after someone has shared.

Repeat this until everyone has shared.

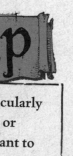

pit·tip

In all activities, particularly those including prayer or public speaking, you want to provide for a range of levels of involvement. Some students would prefer to watch and some will want to be the center of attention. You can encourage both by offering alternatives within any given activity, such as, "If you don't have a lot to share, maybe just say a phrase that summarizes what you're thinking about." In small group activities, the group can choose one person to present to the larger group, allowing the extroverts to come out. Try to avoid putting a student on the spot by calling on someone to pray, read, or speak without warning.

CLEANING UP

Here are some additional open-ended, thought-provoking questions. Use all or some of them to complement—or even replace—the debriefing questions for any of the activities in this study. You can guide students through this section all together, or form smaller discussion groups for more intimate dialogue.

· **What do you think of John's view of God in heaven?**

· **Why is it important to know that God is stronger than the kings of this world?**

· What kind of justice can we hope for when we believe in God?

· When is it OK to be like Daniel, even if it means disobedience?

· How does the discussion of John's day and age change the way you think about the book of Revelation?

· How do you think John's audience responded to his letter?

· How has Jesus comforted you in your own times of need or suffering?

· How might God use you to encourage others when they hurt?

· Who in the world today might be going through the same kinds of things as John's audience back then?

· How will you actually reach out to help others find hope?

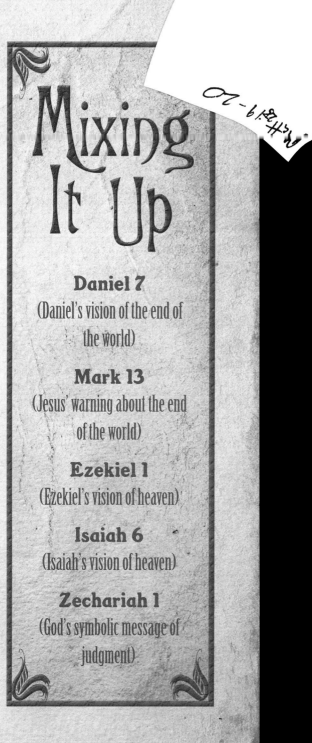

Mixing It Up

Daniel 7
(Daniel's vision of the end of the world)

Mark 13
(Jesus' warning about the end of the world)

Ezekiel 1
(Ezekiel's vision of heaven)

Isaiah 6
(Isaiah's vision of heaven)

Zechariah 1
(God's symbolic message of judgment)

Returning to the Lions' Den

DANIEL

7:13 "As my vision continued…I saw someone like a son of man coming with the clouds of heaven."

10:5 "I looked up and saw a man dressed in linen clothing, with a belt of pure gold around his waist."

7:9 "His clothing was as white as snow, his hair like purest wool."

10:6 "…and his eyes flamed like torches."
"His…feet shone like polished bronze, and his voice roared like a vast multitude of people."

10:10, 12 "Just then a hand touched me…
Then he said, 'Don't be afraid…'"

REVELATION

1:7 "Look! He comes with the clouds of heaven."

1:12-13 "I saw…someone like the Son of Man."
"He was wearing a long robe with a gold sash across his chest."

1:14 "His head and his hair were white like wool, as white as snow."
"And his eyes were like flames of fire."

1:15 "His feet were like polished bronze refined in a furnace, and his voice thundered like mighty ocean waves."

1:17 "But he laid his right hand on me and said, 'Don't be afraid!'"